PENGUIN BOOKS

Will Mummy Be Coming Back for Me?

Will Mummy Be Coming Back for Me?

SHANE DUNPHY

PENGUIN BOOKS

PENGUIN BOOKS

Published by the Penguin Group
Penguin Books Ltd, 80 Strand, London WC2R ORL, England
Penguin Group (USA) Inc., 375 Hudson Street, New York, New York 10014, USA
Penguin Group (Canada), 90 Eglinton Avenue East, Suite 700, Toronto, Ontario, Canada M4P 2Y3
(a division of Pearson Penguin Canada Inc.)
Penguin Ireland, 25 St Stephen's Green, Dublin 2, Ireland (a division of Penguin Books Ltd)
Penguin Group (Australia), 250 Camberwell Road, Camberwell, Victoria 3124, Australia
(a division of Pearson Australia Group Pty Ltd)
Penguin Books India Pvt Ltd, 11 Community Centre, Panchsheel Park, New Delhi – 110 017, India
Penguin Group (NZ), 67 Apollo Drive, Rosedale, North Shore 0632, New Zealand
(a division of Pearson New Zealand Ltd)
Penguin Books (South Africa) (Pty) Ltd, 24 Sturdee Avenue,
Rosebank, Johannesburg 2196, South Africa

Penguin Books Ltd, Registered Offices: 80 Strand, London WC2R ORL, England

www.penguin.com

First published 2009
This edition published for Index Books Ltd 2010

6

Copyright © Shane Dunphy, 2008
All rights reserved

The moral right of the authors has been asserted

NOTE: *The names of people and places mentioned in this book have been
changed where it was felt necessary to protect the identity of individuals*

Set in 11/13.5 Monotype Bembo
Printed in England by Clays Ltd, St Ives plc

ISBN: 978-1-844-88211-3

www.greenpenguin.co.uk

Penguin Books is committed to a sustainable future
for our business, our readers and our planet.
The book in your hands is made from paper
certified by the Forest Stewardship Council.

For Darren. I miss you, brother

Sometimes I feel like a motherless child
A long, long way from home.

Sometimes I feel like I'm almost gone;
Like I'm all alone.

Who's got a shoulder when I need to cry?
I feel restless and I don't know why.
I cry for help, but my calls echo on —
Lord, I'm lost; I can't find my way back home.
My soul is so weak, but I want to be strong;
I try to run away, but I've been running too long . . .

'Motherless Child' (traditional blues song)

NOW

I was aware of several things happening at once, but time had slowed to a crawl, and the world was not making sense.

A boy was standing at the far end of the long conference room in Dunleavy House, shouting at me, but his words seemed to be playing at the wrong speed, and all I could hear was white noise. Mrs Munro, the middle-aged woman who worked, among other things, as the secretary and receptionist for the Dunleavy Trust, the voluntary agency with whom I was employed, was lying sprawled on the large dark wood table. She wasn't moving. I gathered that the youngster had hit her, and might have hurt her badly. This, more than anything else, drove home to me the dire seriousness of the situation: Beverly Munro was a woman who elicited fear in almost everyone, and it took a long time to see the warmth and intelligence behind her gruff façade. The children who came in and out of Dunleavy House – and not a few of their parents and carers – treated Mrs Munro with grave respect. She expected – and demanded – no less.

Ben Tyrrell, my boss, a man with many years' experience of working with the most challenging and damaged children, was trying to wrestle himself from my grip. He was yelling at the top of his voice at the agitated youngster. In all the years I had worked with Ben, I had never seen him so enraged with a child. I knew he and Mrs Munro had been working together since before I was born, and

3

that Ben loved her dearly as a colleague and friend. I'm slightly bigger than Ben – and twenty years younger – and I had managed to get my arms under his oxters, but his distress was lending him strength, and I did not know for how long I could restrain him.

I felt like reality had been tipped upside down. I had worked in environments that were often chaotic and frightening. I was used to that – in truth, I relished it, at times. My job was challenging and interesting, and gave me the opportunity to test my limits on a daily basis. Even though we regularly had troubled people in Dunleavy House – we supervised access visits, as well as holding case conferences and therapy sessions – these were all expertly managed, with specially laid-down rules and guidelines. Boundaries were clear, and even if things went wrong, there were safety measures in place to accommodate the fallout; if extra staff were needed at any of these daily fixtures, they were made available, and any of the rest of us who were in the building made sure to keep an ear out if trouble was expected.

This was a situation outside our normal experience. A youngster in his mid-teens (I put the boy at maybe sixteen years of age) had arrived unannounced at reception late that afternoon, demanding to speak to someone. Mrs Munro had asked him a few standard questions – the name of his social worker, if he was living at home or with foster parents, whether or not he was in school – and she had then shown him into the conference room, while she checked to see if anyone was available to have a chat with him.

On finding that everyone was busy, Mrs Munro had returned to see if an appointment could be made for the following day.

'I'll wait here,' the boy retorted.

'You could be waiting for a couple of hours,' he was told, gently.

'I need to see somebody, and it won't keep until tomorrow.'

'I understand but . . .'

'You tell them I'm going to stay right here until someone comes and talks to me. I've been told youse help people no one else can help. Well, they're gonna lock me up, and that ain't goin' to happen. I want to speak to somebody – right?'

Mrs Munro had sighed, but went and informed Ben that the visitor was refusing to leave. It seemed that, when Ben came out of his office (he had been dealing with a foster mother in crisis) to reason with the young man, things had not gone well. Mrs Munro had somehow got caught in the crossfire. The shouting had alerted me to the situation, and I arrived from my own office, where I had been writing a report, just as Ben was about to vault the table and throttle Mrs Munro's assailant.

My mind raced. Ben was the person I turned to when things were out of control. I expected him to always be calm, to be capable of dealing with anything, regardless of how extreme. To see him in such a state was simply horrifying for me. I wanted to walk away and pretend none of it was happening. I took a deep breath, and forced myself to take stock of the situation. The youngster had picked up a chair, and was brandishing it at us.

'I'll fuckin' do the lot of yiz!' he shouted. 'Try and stop me if you think you're hard enough! You know what I can do if I'm pushed.'

'You need to put that down and talk to me,' I said, loudly, but with as gentle a tone as I could muster. Ben

5

was relaxing somewhat, and I loosened my grip. When I did, he sagged and sat down against the wall. 'What's your name?'

The boy suddenly seemed uncertain. He was not tall, probably only five foot four or five. His hair was shaved close to his head, and his acned face was pale and pinched, betraying a life of hardship. He wore a scuffed and filthy hoody and baggy blue tracksuit bottoms.

'Don't you know me, man?' he asked.

I almost laughed. Was this one of those young gang members so often featured in the papers, convinced his thuggery had made him famous? Was I supposed to have heard of his drug-addled exploits?

'No, I don't know you.'

Something flitted across his face then that I thought I did recognize. It was only momentary, and if my senses had not been heightened through stress, I might have missed it. But the look of pain, of fear, the expression of desolation, leaped out at me like a signature I'd read time and again.

'Jesus, Shane. You have to remember.'

I struggled, then. Childcare workers who claim they remember every child they encounter are liars. We recall many, but just as many are forgotten, filed away in our memories like dreams or snatches of overheard conversations. Some we carry with us, like tattoos or talismans. Others, unknown, carry us with them. It is the nature of the job.

'Help me,' I said. 'Help me remember.'

'His name is Jason Farrell,' Mrs Munro said, then, her voice surprisingly firm.

I had not noticed her pushing herself upright. A bruise was already rising on her cheekbone, but she did not falter, or even cast a glance at the boy, who was now gazing at me, trembling. Slowly, she walked around the table, and went to Ben's side.

'I'm sorry, Beverly,' he said, and I heard him crying. She helped him to his feet. I felt Ben's hand on my shoulder as memory washed over me like a waterfall.

'Jason,' I said. 'My God . . .'

'I didn't know you was here,' he said, and then his face creased up and he was crying loudly and bitterly, like a small child. 'Shane, I'm in trouble, man. Bad trouble.'

I knew I should go to him, but somehow couldn't bring myself to. He had walked into my life and warped it unspeakably. Ten minutes before, I had been calm and happy, doing some mundane paperwork. In less time than it takes to make a cup of coffee, a man I respected and admired had been transformed into a quivering wreck, and a woman I cared for a great deal had been injured. I was too hurt and upset to comfort the perpetrator of these crimes.

So we stood there with the table – and more than ten years – between us: an insurmountable gulf.

'I'm calling the police,' Ben said, his voice gruff with emotion. 'Stay with him, okay?'

'Yeah.'

Jason Farrell was still sobbing when they took him away.

Five hours later I sat opposite Garda Miriam Kelleher in the squad room of the crowded local police station. There was very little floor space, as the room had been packed to capacity with desks and chairs, and the narrow passage-ways that did exist between the workstations were clogged with boxes of files and other assorted detritus.

The sound of the radio crackling into life every few moments punctuated the buzz of conversation.

'He's asking for you,' Miriam said. She was taller than me, with square glasses and dark blonde hair tied in a loose ponytail. She had worked for a time as a residential childcare worker, and therefore caught a lot of the juvenile liaison cases.

'I *will* go and talk with him, Midge, but I need to know what I'm dealing with,' I said. I had drunk too much coffee – even for me – and felt tired and jittery. I wished I was at home, but I knew I wouldn't rest until I had found some answers. The only person who could provide them was locked in a nearby cell. 'I remember this kid as a terrified five-year-old. I'm guessing there's been a lot of water under the bridge since then.'

Miriam pushed a heavy file across her desk towards me. 'Gallons,' she said.

I looked at the ream of paper and sighed, deeply.

'Can't you summarize it for me?'

'Okay, then. In brief, Jason Farrell is about as bad a kid as you could hope to come across,' Miriam said, observing me wince but continuing mercilessly. 'He has been mixed up in a variety of petty crimes, most of them involving violence of one kind or another. It's only a matter of time before he graduates on to something more serious, and someone dies. He's been caught with firearms twice, and we suspect he's on the perimeter of at least one of the local gangs. He's certainly been seen in the company of some of their lower-ranking members.' She sat back and let that information sink in. 'For that alone, I'd be glad to see him put away for a long while.'

'But there's more?' I prompted.

She flipped open the file, and riffled through it to a heavily lined page.

'In 1997, when he was eleven, Jason Farrell took a three-year-old girl, Mary Connors, into a field behind the halting site, an official area for travellers where her family were staying, and molested her. I won't disturb you with the gory details – suffice it to say it was sadistic enough to have him placed in a secure care institution for a year after that. They released him, and put him under the watchful eye of a foster family, but obviously before he was ready. In 1999, he broke into the house of a neighbour, and violently sexually abused their two-year-old daughter.'

'If he's such a serious threat, how come he's still at large?' I asked impatiently. 'Why the fuck is he arriving at my office and beating up my friends?'

'Shane, you'd be the first person to advocate kids getting a second chance, even the really messed-up ones,' Miriam shot back. 'He was put in a programme for young offenders. It seemed to be working, the second time around. He was sent back home to his birth parents in the Oldtown.'

I sighed. 'I can guess that didn't go well.'

'A couple of complaints came in about him hanging around the local primary school,' Miriam said. 'I had a talk with him, that time, warned him off. Then we got a call about a little girl who had been approached by a man when she was out playing. This guy wanted her to go for a walk with him. He said he'd buy her a new doll. Thankfully, she was well aware of "stranger danger", and ran and told her parents. Our boy swears blind it wasn't him, and I won't make a four-year-old pick him out of a line-up, so we let that one lie. But last week, there was a burglary – an old woman who lived in the flats. She was in bed, and when she got up to confront the intruders, one of them dragged her back into her room and sexually assaulted her. This is an eighty-year-old woman, mind. Even though he was wearing a balaclava, she was able to give us enough information to identify Jason.'

'How?'

'Indian-ink tattoos on his hand. Unmistakable. He's going down, this time.'

'He's still only sixteen. That's a child, the last time I looked.'

'He's been kept out of the really serious juvenile detention centres before now. But not any more. He's a serial offender, Shane, and a fucking menace to society. Do you want to see a photo of that old lady's face? He bruised it up pretty good. Bit her cheek so badly she needed stitches. I could give you a description of the genital scarring.'

I shook my head. 'No thanks.'

'He might have only been a pup when you last saw him,' Miriam said, 'but he's grown into a fucking Rott-weiler. There's nothing any of us can do, now, except put him where he isn't a danger to anyone.'

I rubbed my eyes. 'Can I go and talk to him?'

Miriam sat back and put her hands behind her head. I could see her biceps flex beneath her blue shirt. She was a pretty girl, but it would have been a mistake to think that was all she was. 'Are you sure you want to?'

'I guess I owe it to him.'

'Why? What good will it do?'

'Dunno. But it can't hurt, can it?'

She shrugged. 'Your funeral. Come on, then.'

★

Jason was sitting on a thin mattress on the floor of his cell. There was no other furniture, so I closed the lid on the stainless-steel toilet, and sat on that.

'I'll be at the other end of the corridor,' Miriam said, and left us.

'D'you want a cigarette?' I asked.

Jason nodded.

When I had two lit, I looked at him. His eyes were red from crying, and I noticed that his hands were almost completely discoloured from the amount of tattoos he had on them. I thought, momentarily, that he had been stupid not to wear gloves when he had broken into the old woman's house, but dismissed the thought. If he had been stoned or psychotic enough, the reality of getting caught would not have even occurred to him.

'I don't know what you think I can do for you,' I said. 'You've done some pretty bad shit.'

'Remember when you was workin' with me in the home?' There was a childish urgency in his voice. He needed me to remember, as if it somehow validated my being there.

I nodded. 'Yeah, Jason. I remember, now.'

'Them was some good times, wasn't they?'

I ignored the question. He was not the little boy I had known. That child was still there, but buried deep. Sentimentality could be dangerous.

'Why did you come to Dunleavy House?' I asked. 'Was it to see me?'

Jason smiled sadly. 'Naw. I didn't even know you worked there. One o' the lads I knows told me your boss got him out o' juvie. I thought yiz might be able to get me off what I done.'

'What did your friend do?'

'Breakin' and ent'rin'.'

'Jason, you raped an old woman. That's a hell of a lot more serious.' I was viscerally aware that the assault on the elderly lady was only a small part of what this skinny kid had done, but didn't think revisiting his other crimes served any purpose, just then.

'I din' rape 'er! I on'y felt 'er up a bit.'

I stood.

'Where ya goin'?'

'It's long after my clocking off time,' I said. 'I'm not going to sit around and be lied to when I could be at home. I'll see you, Jason. I'd like to say it was nice of you to look me up, but I'm not sure it was.'

'No – don' go. I'm sorry. Okay, what I done was bad. I know it was, okay?'

I sat back down. He relaxed again, when I did. My presence seemed to soothe him. His disturbed me deeply, but I could not allow him to see that it did.

'How come you din' know me?' he asked.

'It was a long time ago, Jason. I've worked with a lot of kids since then, in a lot of places. You look very different.'

'We was tight, though, you an' me. Wasn't we?'

I closed my eyes, and felt the years drop away like dry leaves, and for a moment the tiny cell was no longer there, and it was a summer day in a city far away, the air rich with possibilities.

THEN

Waterford, 1991

I was free.

It was a strange feeling, that sense of utter abandonment. I was, for the first time, a fully qualified childcare worker. I had passed my exams, served my time on a variety of placements, and was clutching my results in my hand as I sat on the grass outside the main building of Waterford Institute of Technology on a spectacularly sunny June afternoon. I had not exactly distinguished myself academically, but I had passed with honours, and was well pleased with myself.

Darren, my best friend and associate, was lounging on the lawn beside me. Students milled about the campus, many carrying bags and suitcases as they said goodbye to their classmates – some for the holidays, some for the last time. Darren, too, had successfully negotiated the final examinations, and was about to embark on a life in child protection, as well. He folded his own results sheet and put it in the pocket of his jeans.

'Fancy a pint?'

I nodded. 'It's cidery weather.'

'It is, that.'

The bar in Waterford Institute is called The Dome (because it has one perched atop it), and it was thronged with students that afternoon, many celebrating, a few drowning their sorrows. Darren secured our drinks – pints of draught cider – and brought them out to the beer garden. I rolled us two cigarettes from a pouch of Samson tobacco, and we sat and watched the world going by.

Darren and I had only known one another for the three years we had been studying, but we had developed a deep friendship in that time, and neither of us felt the need for constant inane conversation. Companionable silence was often what we were happiest with.

We were into our second drink when a man pushed his way through the crowd and approached our table. He was wearing expensive-looking cord trousers and a brightly coloured T-shirt. A stranger to the college might have mistaken him for a student, but he was in fact a senior lecturer in the Social Care Department. His name was Denis O'Shea, and he was the kind of teacher who divided students right down the middle – you either loved or hated him. He was a charismatic person with a powerful ego and steely determination to distinguish himself in his field, and that summer afternoon he was in an expansive mood. When he sat down, he offered no greeting, and Darren and I surveyed him languidly. 'You both look happy,' Denis ventured. 'Or am I mistaking drunkenness for good cheer?'

'We're not drunk yet, Denis me ol' boy, but we do intend to get there,' Darren said, taking a long draught of his pint. 'You are very welcome to join us, but if you so much as attempt to talk shop, I will cheerfully throttle you.'

Denis winked at us slyly. He had a flair for the dramatic. 'I won't mention the telephone conversation I just had, then.'

I raised an eyebrow. 'Have you come to bring us good news or bad news, Denis? Because anything other than good news today will only lead to the pummelling Darren just mentioned, so think carefully about your answer. We're pleasantly mellow here, and you are not to ruin it.'

'I'll tell you what,' our former lecturer said, reaching for the tobacco pouch. 'You buy me a drink, and I'll tell you all about it.'

It was Darren's round, and he shook his head and stood up. 'What'll it be?'

'I'll have a lager.'

'Same again for you, Shano?'

'I'll force another down.'

Denis finally got around to filling us in on his news when we all had full glasses.

'A new residential childcare centre is opening in the city. It's more or less fully staffed, except for one thing: the Health Board requires a quota of male careworkers. Which means there is one position as yet unfilled.'

'Which is where we come in,' I said.

'Do either of you want it?'

'What kind of kids?' Darren asked.

'They're quite young. Smallest is five, I think. There's four of them in all.'

Darren and I looked at one another. 'Teenagers are kind of my speciality,' Darren admitted. 'I don't have a huge amount of experience with tots.'

'I've done some pre-school work,' I admitted. 'But the fucking city, Denis. I live here. My family are all in the South East.'

'Do you want a job, Shane?'

I nodded. 'Is there anything else I need to know?'

'They pay cash money, and they have a vacant position.'

'I'll give them a call. Who's running the show?'

'A woman called Terri. Here's the number.' He took a

crumpled sheet of paper from the pocket of his waistcoat and passed it over to me. I took the details, and didn't think about it again for two days.

I was hung over. The end-of-term celebration had gone on the rest of that afternoon, and well into the night. I was making a humble living as a musician playing for the bus-loads of tourists who passed through Waterford, and had a gig the following afternoon. An enthusiastic group of Americans had insisted on buying me, and the folk group I was playing with, drinks for the entire evening. The gig had turned into a spontaneous sing-song, and the landlord of the pub had surreptitiously locked the door, pulled down the blinds and allowed us to while away the night until the wee small hours. I had got ridiculously drunk all over again, and was now suffering for my bad behaviour.

I was lying in bed, wishing the room would stop spinning long enough for me to climb off when someone banged on my bedroom door.

'Go away,' I moaned.

'Phone,' Darren shouted in. We shared a flat on the Waterford Quays.

'Tell them I moved to Tasmania.'

'Okay.'

It was four in the afternoon before I surfaced. As I sat on the couch trying to force some water down, Darren handed me a scrap of paper with a number scribbled on it in his spidery handwriting. 'She called again around an hour ago. Someone called Terri.'

I nodded, but was immediately sorry I had, and stopped. I awoke from a doze with a start at six. The old-fashioned black phone that sat atop our portable TV was jingling loudly.

'I bet it's for you,' Darren said, picking it up. He listened for a second. 'Yeah, he's just arrived back from Tasmania.' He held out the receiver. 'Terri again.'

I struggled to sit up. 'Hello.'

'Hi. I've got you at last.' The accent was jubilantly Australian.

'You certainly have.'

'Denis O'Shea told me you were interested in a job that has recently become available.'

'Yeah . . . I suppose I am . . .'

'You suppose?'

'No – I apologize. Of course I'm interested.'

'Hey, I don't want to force this on you . . .'

'No. I'm all ears. Tell me about the job.'

'Let me go one better, and invite you to come up and meet me and the kids tomorrow. Unless you have other plans, of course.'

'I should be able to arrange something.'

'Good. We're on Threadgold Place. Near the park. The house is called The Crow's Nest, you can't miss it. Now, I suggest you take some aspirin, drink a couple of gallons of water, and go back to bed.'

The line went dead.

Darren looked over at me. 'She sounds nice,' he said.

'She sounds Australian,' I said, walking stiffly over to put the receiver back in its cradle.

'Australians are nice,' Darren offered.

'I think this one might just be too clever for her own good,' I muttered, and, taking a bottle of water from the fridge, stomped back upstairs to bed. If Terri was to be my new boss, I might as well start taking her instruction.

The Crow's Nest was well named: the building was tall and thin, seemingly containing four floors and looking as if it might topple over in the light breeze at any moment. It was set in its own grounds, which looked like they took up around half an acre, and these were dotted here and there with mature trees, each of which was home to many talkative crows. I surveyed the house from the small park and playground directly across the road, which also echoed with the sounds of cawing rooks and jackdaws. As I watched, a boy and a taller girl of indeterminate age ran from the open front door of the house, and tore helter-skelter around the side. A tall woman with straw-blonde hair emerged from the house moments later, and ran after them. Both she and the kids looked happy and relaxed. It was a good sign.

I had done some work in residential childcare during my college course. As part of our training, we had been expected to work full time in three separate care settings, one of which had to be a residential placement. Residential is the most intense and emotionally tough type of childcare there is, for the simple reason that you are having a true living experience with the children you are caring for: you get up with them in the morning, put them to bed at night (and get up with them in the middle of the night, if needs be), deal with mundane things like homework and dental visits, and more exceptional things like seeing psychologists or bringing them to prison to see incarcerated parents.

I had thoroughly enjoyed my time in res. It had been an experience I was not really looking forward to, as my previous jobs had all been nine-to-five (in theory at least), and as someone who was used to having my evenings free for music or socializing, the thought of antisocial hours, sleepovers and night shifts did little to enamour me to it.

However, it was not long before I realized this kind of work had its own rewards. Being on-site over two days at a stretch meant that I got to see work through with specific children, watching them grapple with the various dilemmas or demons they were facing, and come out the other end. I had the pleasure of reading bedtime stories, of planning birthday parties, of picking out Christmas presents, of attending parent–teacher meetings – as someone just out of my teens, these were all new experiences for me, and ones I took to with great gusto. This was childcare as I had never really experienced it before. I had previously been more in the role of teacher and facilitator, but here I was taking a much more prominent position in the child's life.

That wasn't to say that there were no downsides to this methodology. If a child was having a bad day, or decided to give you a hard time, you were stuck there, right in the firing line, for twenty-four hours or more with no escape route. I also learned rapidly that a sleepover often involved very little sleep. I had had nights when some child or other woke every hour, meaning I slept not one wink.

But these were minor concerns. I found the overall experience joyous and revelled in the sense of team spirit and camaraderie of working so closely, not just with the children, but with my colleagues also. I discovered in residential care a sense of community and a feeling of belonging that I had often craved. Here was a job, a role and a place where you were part of something greater than yourself, and where the work was hugely important. I knew, in a real sense, that we were changing people's lives.

When I look back at myself as I was then, with the cold eye of someone who has passed through much – professionally and personally, and had the benefit of years of reflection and self-analysis – I realize that I was, first and foremost, dangerously underqualified for the job I was proposing to take on. I foolishly believed that my three work placements at college had prepared me for anything I might encounter, and that I was already battle-hardened and initiated into the worst the work could throw at me. When you add to that a ridiculously arrogant personality, and the firmly held conviction that I was just about the best childcare worker there was, you have a recipe for disaster.

If I had known then what I know now about the following twelve months, and the fallout that would come to find me eleven years later, I would have walked away there and then, without looking back.

But, of course, I didn't. I crossed the road, and walked through the open front door of The Crow's Nest.

The house was just as impressive on the inside. The hallway was long and ornate, with a curving, wooden staircase leading off it. The walls were painted in bright, clean colours and decorated with paintings by the children, all professionally framed. Doors led off to a living room and a playroom, and at the end was a large, well-lit kitchen. A high counter with bar stools divided a dining area from the cooking space, which had an artfully designed gas-cooker and oven.

I hallooed and called, and finally a freckled, curly-haired girl in her mid-twenties came down the stairs, and met me in the hall.

'You must be Shane,' she smiled. 'I'm Sarah. I'm to be your work partner.'

'I ... um ... I haven't actually been given the job yet ...' I said, shaking her hand.

'Oh.' Sarah pretended to look abashed. 'Well, I'd better let Terri talk to you. She's out in the garden with Mark and Ellen. I'll call her in.'

Sarah brought me into the kitchen, and sat me down at one of the high stools, then disappeared out of a patio door. She returned with the tall blonde woman I had seen from the park.

'Here he is,' Sarah said. She was leading the two children by the hand, and they eyed me warily. I couldn't blame them. Darren often said that at this time I was going through my 'Serpico' phase, which meant that I looked like a member of the Grateful Dead: my beard was thick and full, and my hair hung halfway down my back.

Terri, on the other hand, did not appear to be fazed one iota. 'Hey,' she said, extending her hand. Close up, I was a little taken aback by her. She was breathtakingly beautiful, in that classic 'surfer chick' kind of way. She was probably close to six feet tall, and her long, almost white, blonde hair, flecked with bits of grass and leaves, was loose and wind-blown from the game of chase. She wore a loose fitting T-shirt and shorts, and leather flip-flops on her feet. She looked healthy and strong and very much someone to be reckoned with. 'I see you made it. I'm not gonna bullshit you, mate, I didn't think you'd show.'

24

I laughed nervously. 'I didn't exactly outdo myself over the phone,' I admitted. 'You caught me immediately after finishing my exams, and there was a bit of partying to be done. I suppose I got caught up in that.'

'Ah, forget about it,' she said, walking over to the fridge. 'I'm having an iced tea. It's an Aussie thing, most of you Irish aren't into it.'

'Ah sure, I'll give it a go,' I said.

'Well, don't say I didn't warn you. You can put some sugar in yours, if you like.'

She placed a frosted jug and two glasses on the counter and sat down opposite me.

'Shane, I need a male staff member, and I'm not going to pretend you're the first person I've spoken to about it. In fact, you're the sixth. I've employed three others in the past month, and none of them have worked out.'

I took a swig of tea. It was cold and delicious. I nodded my appreciation. 'What happened with them?'

'The children here are . . . challenging.'

'Aren't they supposed to be?'

'They are, but challenging is a relative term.'

I grinned. 'I think I can take it.'

Terri threw her head back and laughed. 'Oh, Shane, they've *all* said that. Tell me as much in a fortnight's time.'

'Okay,' I said, not sure how to respond. Her voice seemed to be teetering uncomfortably on the edge of hysteria.

'All right, I suppose we should do some kind of an interview. Come on out into the garden and we'll do a little Q and A.'

The patio doors opened up on to a large back garden. I noted that it had been left as simply lawn, a wide, open space with no fancy adornments. A stone patio held a good-sized wooden table with a blue parasol and comfortable chairs. The sun was blasting from a cloudless blue sky, and I was glad of the shade from the umbrella. Terri produced a tobacco tin from the pocket of her shorts. She began to make a roll-up. I followed suit.

'Can you cook?' Terri asked, licking the gummed edge of her cigarette paper.

'Yes.'

'I don't mean can you do beans on toast and sweet-and-sour chicken using a jar of sauce. Can you *really* cook?'

I lit both cigarettes with my Zippo. 'Terri, I can cook like a sonofabitch, given the opportunity.'

'Plenty of opportunity here. The reason I'm labouring the point is because it's a skill that is lacking in the rest of the team. I even brought someone in to try and teach them, but they don't seem to want to learn.'

'So you're still stuck in the "spaghetti bolognese stage" then?'

'Afraid so.'

One of the major problems in a lot of residential care settings is the food. Because staff are dealing with the day-to-day problems of the children in their care, which are often quite serious and time consuming, cooking something nice tends to be a lesser concern. As a result, the fare served up to both staff and children in group homes is, to a large degree, quite awful. Spaghetti bolognese is *the* classic residential meal, usually swimming in grease and with the pasta overcooked to the point of being sludge. Shepherd's pie is another regular menu item, with the mashed potato topping complete with nice, *al dente* lumps and the mince filling lovely and watery. I had also, even with my short experience at that stage in my career, enjoyed frozen pizza (with the middle still good and icy), chicken curry that more closely resembled thin soup and oven chips that were so hard and brittle they could have been used as bullets by the armed forces.

I'd had the good fortune to have worked on one of my placements with a colleague who had been in the military, and believed that physical care was the first step to gaining a child's trust. He lived by the tenet that an army marched on their bellies, and applied this philosophy to the children he worked with, too. If the basic needs were met (food, clothing, shelter), and met well, then the rest would follow. He insisted that food at his units be well prepared, nutritious *and* tasty. I had seen him arriving in the kitchen at meal times and dumping what had been prepared by a less-than-interested childcare worker into the bin, then rolling up his sleeves and cooking up something simple but delicious for the children within twenty minutes. He had told me once, after a particularly tough shift, when I could think of nothing positive that I had done, that the mashed potatoes I had made for that evening's dinner had been some of the best he had ever tasted. *That*, he said, was something really positive.

'So you want me for my culinary skills. I'm flattered.'

Terri grinned a Cheshire cat grin and put one of her long legs up on the table.

'No ... well, yes, it *had* occurred to me that having a team-member who could actually boil water successfully wouldn't hurt, but there are two main reasons I want you. First, I have to employ a bloke. It's been written into policy that we have to have a ten per cent quota of male childcare staff. That might sound stupid, and I do believe that it is, but it's a fact. The Health Board feels it is essential to have a gender balance. To be honest, these

27

kids are so challenging right now, the gender of their carers doesn't matter a damn, but there you go. I do as I'm told. You, matey, have a penis, so you are therefore qualified for the position.'

'It's a good thing I'm not sensitive,' I said. 'And the second reason?'

'The second has a name. Jason Farrell. He's arriving next week, which will give us our full quota. Besides you, I've recently taken on another four workers – we have six employed here now. Jason has just been taken into care, and I believe he's going to offer the team here their greatest challenge to date.'

'In what way?'

'To be quite honest, I don't know. Information is sketchy. The file I have been given amounts to about five pages, three of which have been written by a part-time family support worker who saw the family once a week. Her writing style is quite minimalist. Obviously an avid fan of Beckett.'

'So what can you tell me?'

'Shane, this is in strictest confidence. You still haven't indicated whether or not you're on board.'

'Well, let's just say I have one foot on the platform, but the other is definitely on the train.'

She grinned and sipped her tea. 'I'll share what I have been able to piece together. Jason is five years old. There is one older sibling, Timmy, who is fifteen, and who remains with his parents. Jason was taken into care one month ago, when a girl in the locality, which is quite rural, rang the police to say that she believed Jason and Timmy were being sexually abused by their father. When the police called social services, and when they arrived at the house, they found Jason locked up in a rear bedroom.

He was naked, and from the stench and the faeces on the floor, it looked as if he had been there for several days. He was dehydrated, undernourished and bore marks of severe physical abuse. He also had to be restrained, as he attacked his rescuers with remarkable ferocity. The parents, Conor and Elizabeth, were questioned, but they actually blamed the brother, Timmy, claiming he insisted on taking responsibility for disciplining Jason. Timmy corroborates the story. Needless to say, this was taken with a pinch of salt, and Jason was placed in emergency care immediately. Unfortunately, the centre he is in is unable to cope with his particular ... er ... foibles. He is apparently holding both staff and children to ransom. Hence, the move to The Crow's Nest.'

'I take it you've met him.'

'Several times. He is what you'd expect, in many ways. Small for his age, very thin. He *can* use the toilet, but will, without thinking, squat and relieve himself on the floor. He's very aggressive, uses teeth, nails and weapons if he can lay hands on anything useful, indiscriminately. He *can* be incredibly affectionate and does seem to want to bond. The problem, of course, is that in the past, physical affection was obviously a part of some form of sexual contact, so hugs and cuddles often degenerate into outright groping. The staff at his current location have had to be very careful. And speech is a problem.'

'Bad language?'

'No language at all. Jason is an elective mute.'

'How do you know it's elective?'

'Timmy and the parents say he can and does talk. But since being taken into care: *nada.*'

We drank our tea and smoked for a time. I could hear children in the park across the street, and a blackbird sang in a tree to our right. A bee buzzed lazily in the honeysuckle that grew in the bushes by the wall. It was a beautiful place, and I was already beginning to feel comfortable and at ease in Terri's company. *I could*, I thought, *see myself liking it here*.

'And you have three other children here already?'

'Yes. Ellen is thirteen and is schizophrenic. She comes from a very neglectful background. She is, I believe, a deeply intelligent young lady, but has regular visual and auditory hallucinations that she often finds terrifying. She can be very violent, to herself and others. She also has problems developing relationships. She has serious trust issues.

'Mark is fourteen, he has Asperger's Syndrome, a high-functioning type of autism. He is also dyspraxic: his intellectual and physical functions aren't properly aligned, so he tends to appear very clumsy and awkward. He's fine so long as furniture isn't moved and things are tidied up and not left in the middle of the floor. He was terribly physically abused by both parents, who believed he was simply a stupid and naughty child. He was taken into care when he was seven, and has moved from setting to setting since then. He was not diagnosed with these disorders until he came here, so he spent a good deal of that time very angry and very confused. Two years ago he sexually assaulted a younger boy in a foster placement he was in. He has received counselling, but he's still going through something of a sexual identity crisis, and he needs to be watched. He's the eldest child here, and he's not small. We try to get him to talk about any desires he has, so we can head them off at the pass, so to speak.

'And finally, little Leo. Leo is our foundling. He was left in a cardboard box on the steps of a church when he was three weeks old. No note, no forwarding address. He's ten now, and he was, in infancy, diagnosed as being Down's Syndrome. To be honest, Shane, if he's Down's then I'm George Bush. I see none of the physical traits. But he does have a speech impediment and testing shows that he has an IQ very much in the lower ranges. I have no confidence in these ridiculous tests and quizzes, Shane me old mate. There are some intellectual areas where he is behind: he struggles with maths, for example. He has been very violent in the past, I believe, primarily, through frustration. There is actually a very complex mind at work, once you dig through the layers of emotional damage he has sustained. A lifetime in care has not been kind to him. But let me tell you, he has a remarkable sense of humour, and a remarkable grasp of language.

'And that, Shane, if you don't count the ghost, is our little group.'

'Ghost?'

'Yeah, The Crow's Nest is supposed to be haunted — the Red Lady, they call her. Daughter of a bloke who owned the place back around the time of the civil war, 1920s anyway. The previous owners swore they saw her all the time. Stuff and nonsense, if you ask me.'

'Very interesting.'

'Oh, it's nothing if not interesting. You won't be bored, here, I'll tell you that. Are you in?'

'What are the hours?'

'We're trying out a new timetabling system. You'd do two shifts a week, each involving a sleepover, eight-till-eight. One extra, shorter, floating shift once a month, to allow you to work with different staff. Two people on at all times, with three if difficulties are expected. I'm super-numerary. I'm here as I see the need.'

'Key-workers?'

Usually in residential childcare, each child has a key-worker, meaning that one member of the staff team takes special responsibility for that child, attending parent–teacher meetings, shopping for birthday gifts, accompanying the child to parental access visits and generally being the significant adult in the child's life.

'Of course. You'll have Jason, when he arrives.'

I nodded. 'Okay. I suppose I'm in.'

'Excellent.'

Terri punched me on the arm, grinning from ear to ear. 'When can you start?'

4

Jason Farrell arrived at The Crow's Nest the following Tuesday. It was noon when the car that he was travelling in pulled into our driveway, and the heat was already causing the tarmacadam to shimmer on the roadway. I stood at the front door with Terri and my new partner, Sarah.

The staff system Terri operated encouraged the development of very close professional relationships, and it offered the children a sense of stability and permanence.

Sarah was petite, freckled, and had brown eyes and a gentle but purposeful way of speaking that seemed to command attention. She had a broad range of experience in a number of different care fields, being qualified in mental-handicap nursing as well as mainstream childcare, and she had just returned from doing relief work in the Congo. I liked her immediately. Sarah's temperament suited me perfectly – she was quiet, thoughtful and conscientious. She analysed everything and had a sense of humour that sometimes verged on the funereal. She did not seem at all put out about being teamed up with a male worker, which was always a worry in social care.

Sarah and I had agreed to a policy of honesty: as we were to be living together *at least* two days a week for the foreseeable future, we would need to be able to speak openly. If she did anything that pissed me off, I had to feel free to say it, and vice-versa. In childcare, free speech is vitally important. It is actually the little things that can destroy a team.

The driver door of the car opened and Yolanda Morris, a social worker, got out. She waved at us, and opened the rear door – she obviously had operated the child lock for the drive over. Very slowly, as if movement itself caused pain, a small, dark-haired boy climbed out of the back of the car, helped by Yolanda. He was dressed in ill-fitting clothes of dull colours, but it was his face that drew my attention: even though I knew he was only five, it was lined and seemed almost old. His eyes, when he looked up at us, were dark and emotionless. He held Yolanda's hand in a loose grip, and wrinkled his nose, as if he could smell something bad.

Jason had a strange posture – he stood in a stooped, slightly ape-like manner, with knees bent and shoulders distinctly rounded. His hair was quite long and shaggy, and he peered out at the world through a dense fringe that needed either to be combed out of his eyes or cut. The past month could not have been easy on him, and the pressure was beginning to tell. I felt a mixture of fascination and pity for this waif.

Yolanda led him up to our assembled group.

'Jason, I'd like you to meet some new friends,' she said, using a sing-song tone as she spoke to them.

Many people, even seasoned professionals, lapse into what I call 'the childcare voice' when talking to children. It is not a normal way of speaking. It is usually high-pitched, babyish, patronizing, and seems to work on the premise that children are somehow of lesser intelligence than the rest of the population. It annoys me a great deal. Children, even very young children, are people, and deserve respect. You would not talk to your doctor or lawyer as if they were idiots, even if they actually were. The same courtesy should be afforded to children.

'Hi, there, Jason,' Terri said, extending a hand.

The boy did not move for a moment. He peered up at Terri through his mane, then lowered his gaze until it was aimed at the extended hand. I wondered if he was going to sniff at the fingers, but instead he took Terri's hand and turned it over to examine the palm.

'My name is Terri, and I want to welcome you to The Crow's Nest.'

Jason darted a look up at Terri, held her gaze for a moment, and then returned his attention to the grooves of her palm.

'Do you know what a crow's nest is, Jason?'

The boy gave no sign he had heard Terri speak. She continued, unfazed. 'It's a place on a ship that is high, high up, from where the sailors can look ahead and see what's coming. I think that's a good way of thinking about this house, too. While you live here, you'll be a part of everything we do. If there are plans to be made, you'll be a part of them; you'll know what's coming, just like the sailors. At The Crow's Nest you will never be hurt, or frightened or put at risk, by me or by any of the people who work here. Other children live here too, and we expect them to treat you with kindness and respect, and for you to treat them in the same way. There aren't any rules here, just that you treat everyone the way you would like to be treated.'

This speech was met with silence and apparent in-difference from Jason, who had stopped looking at Terri's fingers, and had turned his back to us all completely, and was now gazing in the direction of the park, where the sounds of children playing could be heard.

'This is Shane and Sarah,' Terri said, nodding at us to take over.

'Hi, Jason,' I said, squatting on my haunches so I was level with him, but keeping a distance so as not to invade his personal space. 'I'm Shane. I've just started here too, so maybe we can help each other settle in.'

Jason had turned back around and he moved over, reached out a hand and, quite gently, touched my hair. He rubbed it between forefinger and thumb. He did not look at my face, but instead focused on the lock of hair as if it was all of me that existed. He had not made a single sound since getting out of the car.

'Yeah, my hair's kind of long all right,' I said. 'You seem to find that strange. Your dad and your brother, they have short hair?'

Jason looked at me pointedly, as if I had crossed a line, and suddenly gave my hair a vicious tug, and then stepped back to Yolanda.

'Ow,' I said, rubbing my head and standing up.

'Now, Jason, no hurting,' Yolanda scolded. 'We've spoken about that. That's not the way to do things.'

I was uncertain how to respond. I didn't want to come the heavy with the boy seconds after he had arrived, but I also did not want to immediately set a precedent for aggressive, cruel behaviour, either. I knew Jason was telling me to back off, that my overtures weren't wanted. The act was designed to say that he was self-contained, and did not need any of us.

I could not let it pass, however.

Jason was glowering at me, his teeth bared and a look of absolute determination etched on to his young face. *Come on*, that look was saying, *just try me*. Terri was waiting for me to deal with the situation. She was looking over at me with a gentle smile on her face.

'Jason,' I said, squatting down again, 'I'm going to let

that go, because you've just arrived and you have to get used to how we do things. But I just want you to know that, like Terri said, we don't hurt one another here.'

Jason swung at me with his nails bared like claws and I moved slightly aside so that he missed. It wasn't a serious attempt to hit me, more a shot across my bows, but I stood up quickly, nonetheless. He was a live one. No doubt about that.

'I'm Sarah,' my partner said, smiling, but sensibly staying where she was. 'I'm very pleased to meet you.'

Two almost-black eyes glanced at her, but there was no response.

'Well, let's go on in and meet the others,' Terri said, smiling at Yolanda and her tiny charge. 'And I'm sure you're both hungry after your drive?'

That elicited the first positive expressions. Jason didn't smile, but his countenance became less adversarial.

'Well, we've got some sandwiches and lemonade waiting, and I bet you'd like to see your room.'

Jason remained where he was, holding Yolanda back.

'Come on, then! What are we waiting for?' she asked. Finally, with a barely perceptible nod, the boy moved forward.

Terri led the way into the house. Yolanda followed, ooing and aahing at everything she saw, as if the place was Disneyland.

'What do you think?' Sarah asked, grinning at me.

'I think that life is about to get very entertaining,' I said.

We went inside.

Sarah and I had spent the morning making sandwiches of various denominations, and I had also made a large jug of fresh, iced lemonade. Terri and the other children had done a good job of laying the table in the dining room, and the previous night a colourful banner reading WELCOME JASON had been made and was hung rather precariously on the wall.

Ellen, Mark and Leo were lined up by the kitchen door to meet their new housemate. They were dressed in their best clothes, were clean and combed and, for that moment at least, were on their best behaviour. They were a motley trio. Ellen was tall and thin, with a mop of red hair and an angular, fragile face. Her eyes were always on the move, never resting in one place for long, as if she was expecting to be attacked from any angle at any moment. Her body was a mass of twitches and jerks. It seemed that she was never at rest.

Mark was also tall, and had the looks and physique of an athlete. He had blond hair that he wore in a crew cut, and his face could have been carved by Michelangelo. Closer inspection, however, revealed that something was not quite right. There was a peculiar angle in the way he stood, an odd glint in his eye, perhaps. In truth, it was nothing anyone would have been able to put their finger on. Mark was, simply, a bubbling cauldron of neuroses and pathologies. Terri suspected that he had been abused while in one of the many institutions he had spent time in over his seven years in care, and this, combined with his autism and dyspraxia, had created a deeply disturbed, troubled boy.

Leo was much smaller than his two peers. Ten years old, but quite capable of passing for six, a mass of curls sat atop a head that looked too big for him. In fact, his entire body appeared to have been constructed from spare parts. His nose was constantly running, and the smell of faeces seemed to drift around with him, as his bowels never functioned properly. One leg was shorter than the other, and his shoes had to be specially made to compensate. A pair of thick-lensed glasses perched crookedly on his face, and one of his eyes strayed off to the left. When he spoke, he slurred his words, as if his tongue did not fit into his mouth comfortably, and consequently he drooled all the time. It was this that had caused Leo to be labelled as Down's Syndrome – children with that disorder have mouths that are too small to hold a normal tongue. Leo, however, was *not* a child with Down's Syndrome, but he did have an array of congenital defects that suggested to us that he was the result of several generations of intrafamilial breeding. I had, though, in the short time I had been around him, already developed a genuine affection for the child. Terri was right: his appearance gave the impression that Leo was profoundly intellectually disabled, but he was, in fact, a very bright little boy with a wicked sense of humour and an appetite for fun that could not be contained.

Ellen, Mark and Leo were obviously expecting to be formally introduced to the new arrival, but they were disappointed. Jason completely ignored them and made a beeline for the food. Terri watched him with a wry grin for a moment, and then cleared her throat.

'Jason, would you mind holding on for a moment while you meet the lads?'

Jason paused, his mouth full and a sandwich in each hand, and none too happy with this turn of events. He was breathing heavily through his nose, his mouth full to absolute capacity, egg mayonnaise and bread spilling out of the corners. Finally, he stuffed the sandwiches he was holding into his pockets.

'That's better. Now, this is Ellen.'

''lo,' she said.

'Mark.'

'How are ye doin'?' he said nervily.

'And Leo.'

'Ith great to meet you. Thave thome food for the retht of uth, though, righ'?'

'Very nice,' Terri said. 'Now, let the festivities commence.'

Jason dived right back into the food. Our own three looked at us with dubious expressions and moved around the table, attempting to get a couple of sandwiches before they completely disappeared. This was no easy job. Jason was absolutely determined to cram as much into himself as was physically possible, and obviously intended to hoard the rest. Within seconds Leo had been elbowed in the nose, Ellen's foot had been stamped on to distract her from getting a glass of lemonade, and Mark had lost his temper and shouted a mouthful of colourful invective at the dark-haired dervish of destruction. Mealtimes needed to have some kind of order, as far as Mark was concerned. Asperger's Syndrome is a very mild form of autism, but it is autism just the same. Mark had his own place at the table, a personal plate, a special glass and an individual knife, fork and spoon. If we were eating informally, as we were at that moment, he insisted that people take turns, that the plate be passed around at regular intervals and that boundaries of space be respected – he *hated* people reaching across him. This lunchtime was a nightmare for Mark, and I could see him getting more and more agitated. Jason was also aware that the tension was rising, and seemed determined to keep the pressure on. I could see him glancing slyly about, purposely shoving against Mark, and trying to make him spill his drink. The last straw was when Jason actually grabbed a sandwich from Mark's plate. Mark howled and lunged at him, trying to grab the smaller boy by the throat. Jason uttered the first sound I had heard him make: he squealed with glee and shot under the table, sitting there munching the purloined snack contentedly. Mark, not to be so easily dissuaded from a course of action, dropped to the floor to follow, but Sarah, like a shot, grabbed his leg and hauled him back. Terri was down on the floor beside him in a second, an arm wrapped around his shoulders.

'Hey there, Mark,' she said gently. 'Come on now, you know better than that. Let's all just settle down and take some time out, shall we? Look, while Jason is having his party under there, why don't you take a few sarnies and retire to the lounge? It'll be nice and quiet in there, and you can stick on one of your *Star Trek* videos? How's that sound?'

Mark looked at her and nodded, casting one final grim glance at the smirking Jason.

'Okay, Terri, but I don't think I'm going to like that guy. He's rude.'

'Whooeee,' Jason shouted after him. He giggled throatily and tore a chunk from the sandwich.

'While you're down there, I'm goin' to eat all the other thandwiches,' Leo called down to him, trying hard not to laugh.

'Jason, I'd really appreciate it if you'd come out and join the rest of us,' Terri said, as Sarah led a still fuming Mark out of the room, with a plate of sandwiches and a glass of lemonade on a tray.

Jason was laughing loudly and spraying bread and sandwich filling over us as we crouched down to him. As

I watched, he emptied his glass all over the floor and belched loudly.

Terri smiled back at him as if he had just offered to do the washing up.

'Well, if you're more comfortable where you are, mate, you just stay there. I'll get you a cloth. You seem to have spilled something.'

The boy's face changed to one of complete puzzlement. Terri wasn't being cross with him – there was no tone of antagonism, just gentle firmness. I tossed a dishcloth over from where I was standing, by the sink.

'There you go.'

Terri handed it to the still dumbfounded Jason.

'Now, young man.'

Jason, still without comment, put his plate and his empty glass on the floor and slowly reached over to the puddle he had created. He dabbed at the pool awkwardly, and when the towel had absorbed most of it, cast a glance at Terri, who was watching him with a neutral expression on her finely boned face. Before she could move, and with pinpoint accuracy, Jason flung the sodden towel, and hit her square in the forehead. He cackled heartily, and thumped the floor with his heels.

'Oh my,' Yolanda said.

'Will I get the broom?' Leo asked helpfully. 'We can drive him out of there with it.'

'No, Leo. He'll come out when he's good and ready,' Terri said.

'He's really weird,' Ellen whispered, trembling slightly and picking at her sleeve. 'I don't like him.'

'Why don't you like him, Ellie?' Terri asked her, placing an arm around her skinny shoulders.

'He . . . he doesn't speak, but he makes a lot of noise.

42

And he smells funny. And he has mad eyes. I . . . I think that he can send evil thoughts out of them. Like poison.'

Silence reigned under the table, as Jason listened to this. It must have been hard for him to hear, but there was no point in censoring the children's thoughts. If they didn't say it now, they would say it later. Kids have a sometimes devastating honesty that will not be quashed by etiquette.

'Well, honey,' Terri said. 'Nobody can send evil thoughts. We can all think bad things about people, but those thoughts stay inside us unless we speak them out loud. And do you remember when I met you first? You didn't smell too good, did you? Because you had to learn about looking after yourself. But look at you now.' She took a deep, theatrical sniff. 'You smell fresh as a daisy!'

Ellen laughed, blushing.

'And as for noisy – well, my dear, you can make quite a bit of noise when the mood takes you. We don't really mind loudness here, do we? This is a place where we can all be just who we are, and that can sometimes mean that there's a little bit of shouting and crying and laughing and whatever else we want to do. Isn't that right?'

Ellen nodded.

'I s'pose you're right.'

'Well, then, there's no problem, is there? Our new friend will just have to take some time and settle in. All right, I think we've all had enough to eat. How's about we clear up and go to the playroom for a bit of free-time?'

'Yeah!' Leo said.

Ellen smiled and began to pick up the dishes.

Sarah leaned against the counter beside me, and sighed deeply. Jason was cooing under the table like a manic

43

pigeon. 'Entertaining might not be the half of it,' she whispered.

'I always had a flair for understatement,' I said.

Free-time usually happened after lunch, although the timetable was not rigidly laid down. Terri insisted that everything be flexible. As she had said, she wanted the children to feel secure that they knew what was going to happen next, but not to be dependent on it. Every now and again, instead of doing whatever was the next set activity, she would spring something new and interesting on us: a trip out somewhere or a treasure hunt in the garden, maybe. She encouraged the team to do the same, and it kept the children open to fresh ideas and experiences.

Free-time involved the group spending three-quarters of an hour in the playroom. During this time, no guidance was given whatsoever as to what could or should be done. Each child had to decide for him or herself what they wanted to do; there was only one proviso – it could *not* be a video game. In 1991 the Xbox and PlayStation were still in development in their respective laboratories, but the Super Nintendo and the Sega Mega Drive were ubiquitous, and our children were as susceptible to their lurid charms as any others.

The aim of the free-time exercise was to encourage the children to act on their own initiative. One of the many pitfalls inherent in residential childcare was the fact that children are shepherded from one activity to another, their entire lives mapped out for them. They are told when to get up, when to eat, when to watch TV, sometimes even when to go to the bathroom. For this forty-five minutes, at least, they had to decide what to do for themselves.

The playroom was extremely well equipped. It had all the toys required for therapeutic work (a doll's house and figurines to go in it; a sand and water tray; paper and paints; a vast array of story books, traditional fairy-tales as well as more contemporary texts; modelling clay and Play-Doh; toy cars and trucks; a dress-up corner with all sorts of costumes; a small stereo with a decent CD library of all sorts of different music), as well as some toys that would probably not have been accepted by a play therapist: Terri did not ban the more 'violent' toys like plastic guns or swords. She believed that all children had the need to explore the more aggressive side of their nature, and that these toys offered an outlet for that. She had also hung a heavy bag in the corner, and had provided boxing gloves for its correct use. All of our children, she told me, had experienced violence, sometimes of the most sadistic and horrific kind. It was natural that they should feel the need to lash out. If they could do that in this room, through the medium of play, well then they should be encouraged to do so. Alongside an entire wall of the room there was also an elaborate model town, with a fully functioning model railway and a beautifully rendered farm. This was a project that Terri and Mark, with some input from Leo, had been working on for several months, mainly to help develop Mark's fine motor-skills – the smaller, more delicate movements needed for precise tasks. The result was outstanding, and a tribute to all involved. Ellen found the model incredibly soothing, and would sit for hours watching the various trains going round and round the track. She told me that she could see things in the model, that the little painted plastic figures came alive for her.

46

Looking at the dreamy expression on her face as she gazed at it, I believed her.

Once the plates and glasses had been stacked in the dishwasher and the dining-room floor swept, we all filed into the playroom. Mark rejoined the group, obviously not at all disappointed that Jason was still ensconced under the table. Yolanda remained with him, although Terri assured her he could do no damage in there, as all the cupboards were securely closed and the gas supply was switched off when the cooker was not in use. She suggested that Jason be left to his own devices until he felt the need to renew his association with us.

Leo and Mark made their way directly to the stereo and bickered over which CD to put on. Mark enjoyed loud, thumping heavy rock, while Leo favoured Top 40 pop. Ellen did not care for music at all, so paid no heed to their deliberations. Eventually, as almost always happened, Mark won out. Leo was at the bottom of the house pecking-order. Easygoing and slow to anger, he tended to shy away from arguments, and generally backed down. One of the staff team would usually intervene and try to reach a compromise when such discussions arose, so that he got his way at least some of the time, but that was not allowed during this period. So, we were all treated to the dulcet musical stylings of Metallica, at a fairly enthusiastic volume. Ellen went over to the bookshelves and took down a copy of *The Fairy-Tales of Hans Christian Andersen*. She was fascinated by this book, and read passages from it at least once a day. Her favourite story seemed to be 'Cinderella'. It was easy to see why: the neglect and marginalization of the heroine in that tale must have resonated with her quite profoundly. I wondered if she were waiting for a handsome prince to come on a white charger and take all her pain away, or perhaps for a kind fairy to wave a wand and still the voices in her head. She took the book over to the model town and, switching on the power, set the trains rolling. Satisfied, she settled down on a beanbag and began to read. Mark and Leo took out a box of trading cards they had been collecting and began to play with them. The cards related to a Japanese cartoon series, and the game was absurdly complex and elaborate. The boys had tried to show me how to play it, but I had become confused after five minutes and they had got frustrated with me. Sarah, Terri and I pulled over beanbags and plonked down near the door. We could just about talk over the music.

'Thoughts?' Terri asked.

'Impossible to say at this stage,' I said. 'He's still trying to convince himself that he's tougher than we are, and that we'll be too scared to try and get close. Ask me again in a couple of days.'

'Yeah, he's a sad little boy, isn't he?' Sarah said, watching Leo and Mark play. Every time they pulled a card from their respective decks, they would declare which one it was in a deep, serious voice, just like the characters in the cartoon did. Sarah found this extremely funny, and never seemed to tire of watching them. 'He can't keep that front up for very long. It's as if he's wound up so tightly he'll actually explode. He's ready to spring at the slightest provocation. I mean, Shane got his hair pulled simply because he asked an innocent question. Even the way he examined the hair, it was like it wasn't real to him – a museum exhibit or something.'

'That's a good point, Sarah,' Terri nodded. 'Jason is depersonalizing everyone at the moment. If we aren't real people, we're easier to abuse. He makes hardly any eye contact; his only physical interaction is violence. If he doesn't let us in, we can't hurt him.'

'He's on his guard too, of course,' I added. 'How does he know we won't turn out to be as abusive as his parents? Jason has come out of his corner fighting. He won't accept any kindness. The food was wolfed down, he made no comment, even in terms of body language, on the fact that we had thrown a little party for him or that the kids had made that banner. He's here under sufferance, and I'd guess that he plans to give us all as hard a time as possible.'

'Absolutely,' Terri said. 'In the hopes that we'll send him home. It's the normal reaction for any child under these circumstances.'

'He wants to be sent home?' Sarah asked in disbelief. 'But he's been abused terribly!'

'Yes, by his parents, from what we can gather,' Terri said. 'You know as well as I do that children will love their parents no matter how badly they're treated. Being placed in care is a hugely traumatic experience, even when the child has been tortured abominably. It's like a bereavement. Kids go through the exact same stages as a child does when a parent dies. But you see, when a child is taken into care, the parent is not dead. There is always a chance they can be sent back. So, they will act up terribly in the hopes that they will be returned to the care of the mother or father.'

As Terri was speaking, we all heard a crash, and then a scream from the kitchen. The ejaculation was too deep to have come from Jason. I was closest to the door, and was on my feet and down the hallway before the wail had died in Yolanda's throat. The scene I found in the kitchen was like something from a horror movie, so unreal was it. The social worker was lying on the floor, her skirt hiked at

49

a very undignified angle up about her knees. There was a deep gash carved into her cheek, and blood was puddling on the floor, already congealing on the cold tiles. Jason was holding a shard of broken plate in his hand, and trying to cut Yolanda again. She was doing her best to hold him off, but shock had weakened her, and if I had not grabbed the child about the waist and hoisted him off her, he certainly would have marked the woman a second time.

In a kind of reflex action, he turned to attack me, but I had him about the waist with one arm, and caught his wrist with the other, keeping the pointed piece of pottery away from me. Sarah was there then, and wrestled it from his tiny hand. As she did, Jason Farrell looked deep into my eyes, and I will never forget what I saw in his: there was no love, no innocence, and no vulnerability; they were deep pools of pain and madness. In that moment, I knew that we were dealing with a child who had gone far beyond anything I had encountered in my brief career and, just for a second, I despaired.

NOW

6

Ben Tyrrell looked tired and stressed. His office, usually perfectly ordered and maintained, was a jumble of papers and books – as if he had been looking for something, but had forgotten what it was halfway through the search. Rain beat on the panes of the window, and the moon shone palely from behind scudding clouds.

'He's going to stay with the police for the night, and be moved to St Phelim's in the morning,' I said. St Phelim's was the city's juvenile detention centre. It was where the toughest cases were sent. Many of their children graduated straight from there to the adult prison on Salt Island, or were shipped out to Mountjoy prison, in Dublin.

'Good,' Ben said. 'I hope we never hear from that one again.'

'He has asked for our help.'

'Some are beyond help, Shane.'

I blinked. I had never heard Ben be defeatist before, even with the most extreme cases.

'What the hell is wrong with you, Ben? From the moment this kid walked in here, you've been on edge.'

'What's wrong?' Ben barked, standing up abruptly. 'What's wrong? That little bastard came in here, throwing his weight around as if we owed him something, and then attacked Beverly like she was some . . . some piece of rubbish! I will not allow that behaviour. It will not be tolerated, d'you hear me?'

I remained sitting. I'd always known Ben had a temper.

I had seen him get very angry during case conferences, and had on occasion witnessed him verbally assaulting social workers or psychologists who were making decisions on children based on their own needs rather than the welfare of the child. He and I had clashed from time to time, usually on matters of practice or disagreements about how a case should be managed, but Ben always cultivated an environment where debate was encouraged. I was not afraid to speak my mind to him, and expected Ben to give as good as he got.

'The one and only rule,' I said, reciting something Ben had taught me many years before. 'You don't hurt anybody, including yourself, and you always try your best. I assumed that applied to you, as much as anyone else. And wasn't it you who taught me that there's no such thing as a bad kid? Children are never wilfully bad, you have always maintained up until today; they just make mistakes. I think Jason Farrell came in here and made one motherfucker of a mistake. He's made a lot of them lately. But then, aren't we in the business of helping children make up for their fuck ups?'

Ben sat down again, and buried his head in his hands.

'Want to talk about it?'

Silence. Then: 'No. Thank you.'

I nodded to the top of Ben's greying head, and stood up to leave. When I opened the door, he said: 'I love her, you see. Beverly.'

'I know. We all do.'

'No – you don't understand. She and I are ... well ... together. An item.'

I turned and looked at him. His cheeks were stained with tears, his eyes bloodshot. 'Oh,' I said. 'Jesus, Ben, I didn't know. None of us did.'

'It's not something either of us felt needed to be broadcast.'

'No. Of course not.'

I remained in the door, not sure what to do.

'It just sort of happened. I know that sounds like a cliché, but it's the truth. It started because we were lonely, I think. I was working late, and so was she, and we'd go for a drink or a meal after we locked up. Then, sometimes she'd call at the weekends to chat, and we'd go out for tea. It got so's I'd actually make a point of staying back here after everyone else had gone home, in the hope that she'd stay back too, or she might make a point of dropping in to see if I needed anything. Slowly, it turned into more than just friendship.'

I decided to stay where I was. I knew how embarrassed he was to be telling me this, and I was none too comfortable, either. It was a little bit like walking in on your parents having sex. I saw Ben very much as a kind of surrogate father, and Mrs Munro was so matronly, so much a mother to all the children who came and went, not to mention me and the other workers, it was hard to think of her as anyone's lover. Yet somehow, these two people had found one another, and I was not going to judge them, or begrudge their happiness.

Ben continued: 'Seeing her sprawled on that table, attacked by that thug, it was more than I could stomach. I know I overreacted. I'm sorry, Shane. It was wrong of me to have put you all at risk like that.'

'You didn't put us in any jeopardy, Ben. Shit happens, and we all have to roll with the punches.' The rain and darkness outside seemed to envelop the building in a cocoon. It was like there was no one in existence other than the two of us. It also made Ben's pain all the more palpable. Here was a man who was at the peak of his profession, and who had been forced to face what was, for many careworkers, their ultimate nightmare: to have the horrors our work sometimes unearthed visited upon our loved ones.

There was nothing I could say to make him feel better. He was full of self-doubt, now, and would beat himself a lot more before this was all over.

'Every day, Ben, we make decisions about people's lives. Those decisions can affect their lot for years to come, but we walk away, and move on to someone else, and rarely give it another thought. Today, we both got a dose of reality. You learned that your work and your personal life can't always remain separate, and I learned that the past doesn't go away. I don't know if either of our responses would stand up under close scrutiny.'

'You did fine. And you know it.'

'Did I?'

'Don't milk it, Shane. I freaked out, and there's no way to take that back.'

I shrugged and turned to leave again. 'That all may be true,' I said. 'But we're still left with a kid who needs someone. And I guess I might just have an obligation to be that someone.'

'I don't think I can be impartial here, Shane,' Ben said quietly. 'If you choose to take the case, I can't supervise you. You'd be on your own.'

I stopped, my back to him.

'I'm going to take some time off, I think,' Ben said. 'I'm no good to anyone like this.'

'Call me when you get back,' I said, and walked out, feeling angry and alone.

7

I watched Jason through a two-way mirror. He was sitting in the assessment room of St Phelim's. A psychologist was talking to him. An array of toys, tests and puzzles were spread out on the table between them, and I could see that Jason was being anything but cooperative. I was reminded powerfully of the five-year-old boy he had been – all rage and ambivalence.

'You worked with him before?' Garry Timmons, the unit manager, asked me.

'Long time ago, yeah.'

'In what capacity, if you don't mind my asking?'

'I was his key-worker in a residential unit.'

'How'd that go?'

I laughed bitterly. 'Not well.'

'But you're back on the case?'

'More by accident than design.'

Garry laughed. 'I think you just described this young fella's life there. He has stumbled from one crisis to another, and every now and again fate has caught up with him, and he's had to pay the piper some. This is one of those times, but I'm not at all sure he'll walk away. These are serious allegations. He will go to trial.'

It was midday and the rain had continued unabated. The remand unit was painted grimy, dull colours, as if the staff were making an effort for it to be as depressing as possible.

'What's the likely outcome of that?'

'Well, I don't want to pre-empt anything, but I reckon he's looking at some serious time. He can stay here for another year, but then it's off to an adult prison. The only other possibility is to have him placed on a treatment pro-gramme for sexual offenders. We'd need a family member to vouch for him, and to be prepared to participate in the programme – kind of like a sponsor. He has to be released into a supportive environment, you see. There are other issues at play here, of course. He's been assessed as being ADHD – attention deficit hyper-activity disorder. He has a learning difficulty, too, and there are major anger-management issues. All that needs to be dealt with. This is a very messed-up young man.'

I sat down on a bench beneath the viewing screen and spread my legs out. Garry plonked down next to me.

'I know what you're thinking,' he said. He was as small and thin as Jason, and had a face heavily pocked and scarred from acne. He spoke with a dense inner-city accent.

'Do you?'

'I do.'

'What's that, then?'

'You don't like him being here.'

'Why do you say that?'

'It's a mark of failure on your part that he's ended up somewhere like this.'

I started to object, but he raised a hand. 'Now, before you start trying to plaumause me, don't bother. I know how a lot of people see Phelim's. This is the last stop on the bus before The Joy or The Shaker. And in some cases, you'd be right. But let me tell you, I see lads like your Jason come in here every day of the week. He's in the right place. I want to help him. And I know how to.

If he wants to make a fresh start, I can work with him.'

I nodded, and found tears stinging my eyes. 'He never had a fuckin' chance, Garry,' I said through clenched teeth. 'Not one easy moment his whole life.'

'I know. I really do,' Garry said, gripping my shoulder. 'No one starts out bad. It's the world that turns people that way.'

I fumbled in my pocket for my cigarettes. 'He's done some fucking awful things,' I said as I tapped out a smoke. 'I mean really bad.'

'I know. I know what he's done.'

I cleared my throat and wiped my eyes. 'Should we still be sympathetic in the face of that? I mean, this kid has become what we spend our time fighting against. Hasn't he?'

'If only it were that simple,' Garry said. 'It's not about right and wrong or good guys and bad guys. I'm afraid that a lot of those lines are blurred, and I just stopped finding labels like that useful a long time ago. Jason is a person – he's made some mistakes, and he's hurt some people along the way, some of them badly. It's our job – yours and mine – to help him see that, and start to make his peace, with the world and with himself.'

I stood up, feeling that if I didn't get out of St Phelim's as soon as possible, my head would explode. 'What if he can't do that?'

'Then we just have to accept we came to the game too late to put this one on the right path.'

I nodded and made for the door, the fact that I had entered the fray when Jason was only five years old rebounding in my head like a thunderclap.

8

Karl Devereux slid on to the bar stool beside me and ordered a cup of coffee. He was dressed in a lightweight leather jacket over a charcoal-coloured jumper and dark canvas trousers. His rain-speckled dark hair, tinged at the temples with grey, was worn long and brushed back from his forehead. He was clean-shaven and smelled of sandal-wood.

'Where did you park?' he asked as he took the first sip from his drink. 'I didn't see the Allegro anywhere here-abouts.' Devereux was referring to my classic 1981 Austin car. It was my pride and joy, despite the fact that the Allegros were often referred to as one of the worst lines of motor vehicle ever built. As a car no one had ever really cared for, I always thought it suited me down to the ground.

'It needs a new alternator,' I said. 'It's with my mechanic.'

'Oh. Are you driving a loaner or are you walking?'

'Walking, for the moment.'

I finished my beer and nodded for another. Karl Devereux was a community worker, who had come into social care through a decidedly circuitous route. Growing up on the streets of Black Alley, one of the roughest and most underprivileged parts of Oldtown, he had become an enforcer for one of the local gangs, and finally gradu-ated on to doing freelance explosives work, robbery and strong-arming for whichever criminal enterprise paid him the most. He was eventually sold out by one of his employers, and spent eight years in Mountjoy, Ireland's toughest prison. On his release, he began volunteering for the youth services in the city, and gradually developed a reputation as a skilled, if unorthodox, practitioner. I had come to find his advice and help hugely valuable, and we became good friends.

'So what can I do for you?' he asked.

'Do you know Jason Farrell?'

'Should I?'

I shrugged. 'Thought you might have come across him on your travels.'

'Is he a client of yours?'

'Yeah. He's in Phelim's at the moment, awaiting trial.'

'On what charge?'

I told him.

'You can't protect him from that. He's sixteen, you say?'

'He'll be seventeen in a month.'

'They could hold out and try him as an adult,' Devereux said.

'I'd thought of that.'

'If he's got a long record, they might want to get him off the streets for as long as they possibly can. That would be the most economical way to get the job done.'

'I need to ask you something.'

'Be my guest.'

'It's personal.'

'I may not answer, then.'

'Okay.'

He smiled in the humourless way he had. 'But then, I might.'

I laughed, but it was only a noise. I didn't feel like

laughing, really. 'What made you decide to go straight?'

Devereux looked into his mug, as if the answer might be found in there. 'Ah – that.'

'Jason Farrell has committed dreadful crimes, Karl. But, see, I knew him when he was little, and I saw sides to him that were good – more than good. I have to believe that he can be turned around, but Christ, it's been so long and he's so completely fucked up. Can he be set right?'

'I don't know,' Devereux said, looking at me with his cold blue eyes. 'Every one of us carries around our special, personal demons. We reach an understanding with them in our own, peculiar ways. Your Jason might just be doing that.'

'What changed you, Karl?'

'You're asking a lot,' he said sharply. 'I don't like to talk about it.'

'I wouldn't ask if I didn't need to know,' I said. 'Ben's had to take some time, and no one wants to work with this kid. He burst in and attacked Beverly Munro, and I've got this history with him and . . . it's all fucked up, Karl. I don't know if I can pull him back from the brink. I suppose it would just help to know it's possible.'

'And your logic is that if I could be set on the straight and narrow, anyone can?'

I realized how awful that sounded, but had to admit it was true. 'That's about it.'

'You've got some nerve, I'll give you that.'

We sat quietly for a moment, and I thought he was going to leave. I wouldn't have blamed him. Devereux had, in the past, gone above and beyond the call of duty for me, and he owed me nothing. I knew very little about him – I didn't know anyone who did – beyond the sketchy details of his career, and the small nuggets of information I did have gave little or no insight into the workings of the man's mind. Ben had once said to me that he thought of Devereux as a sort of walking cliché – the criminal come good, determined to give something back to the community, and attacking that task with the same zeal he had applied to his previous, unlawful endeavours. 'It's what makes people so uncomfortable around him,' Ben had said. 'There doesn't seem to be anything behind the desire to do good, and the fact that he sometimes has imaginative and unconventional ways of achieving his ends makes it all the more scary.'

'Prison, for those who make their living from crime, is an occupational hazard,' Devereux said after a few uncertain minutes. 'I had been inside before, for a few months here and a few months there, but never had I been staring down the nose of serious time. It wasn't the building itself that bothered me, or the people who were inside along with me. I had a reputation, and on my second day I very publicly broke the nose of a man who bumped into me in the breakfast line, so I was reasonably confident that I wouldn't be bothered. What concerned me most was the waste of time. You see, people who specialized in my type of mayhem have a shelf life. You have to be prepared to make your money early on, and then get out; disappear, if you can. That last job, which proved to be my downfall, was to be my meal ticket. But there I was: locked up, and without the salary I had been depending on. I had a small nest egg hidden away, but nowhere near enough to set myself up in foreign climes. I had been well and truly done over.'

Devereux's tone was measured and his expression even as he spoke. It was like he was speaking about another person.

'What did you do?' I asked.

'I raged,' he said, simply. 'I was furious, with myself and with my former bosses. I plotted horrible deaths for them; I schemed to wipe them and their entire bloodlines from the face of existence. I lay awake at night, dreaming up outlandish ways of torturing them and humiliating them until they knew my pain and my despair. Every moment I spent behind bars was another testament to the injustice they had done me, and I was determined they would pay, and pay dearly.'

'How long did you feel that way?'

'I would say I was consumed by anger for at least the first two years of my sentence. I found that ire of that magnitude is self-replicating. Constructing scenarios of death and torment for the criminal overlords wasn't enough. I extended my aggression to my mother, and then to my teachers and finally to anyone who had ever wronged me. I went so far as to develop a timeline for my journey of destruction. I reckoned it would take fourteen months to pay back everyone who had hurt me. I was very specific.'

'So what changed your plans?'

'One day I was coming from the showers, when I heard someone screaming. Everyone else walked on, as if nothing was happening. In prison, the last thing you want is to draw hardship like that upon yourself, so people develop a kind of selective hearing. But, see, I was bored, and unafraid, and I wanted to see what was going on. I followed the cries.'

I saw him, in my mind's eye. He was slimmer – thin to the point of skinny, but with a wiry strength about him, and a balanced stride. His hair was wet and tousled from the shower – he had not combed it yet. He carried his wash-kit – safety razor, wash cloth and flip-flops, under one arm, a towel wrapped about his waist. He stepped from the line of marching men, and walked down a short, narrow hall to a dressing room. Inside were three men, two of whom were similarly attired, one naked. A fourth was being held between them.

'Gang rape is a common enough occurrence in any male prison. I suppose it happens in women's jails too; I haven't ever asked about it. The victim's name was Donny. He was a sneak thief and a confidence man who was in for five. He was harmless, gentle, a bit effeminate – an easy target. As I watched, they stuffed a towel into his mouth to stop him shouting. As they did it, he looked at me, straight in the eye. And that, Shane, was my Road to Damascus moment.'

My voice must have been barely audible: 'Why?'

'I had no feelings about Donny either way. I neither liked nor disliked him. I didn't know him. But in that instance, I saw something in his eyes I recognized. This was the first time he had ever been made to feel utterly helpless and alone. He was in a place where nightmares become reality, where you can scream, and no one will come. I had forced a lot of memories out of my head, over the years, made myself forget my past and the awfulness of my childhood. But suddenly, Donny brought it all back to me. I remembered feeling lost and weak. I could see myself at the mercy of people who knew they could use me for their own pleasure and amusement, and who didn't care if I cried.'

'What did you do?'

'I . . . um . . . I extricated Donny from his situation.'

'You beat up the men.'

'Something like that.'

'Did you get in trouble?'

'No. These were not the type of individuals who would inform on someone who had bested them, particularly three to one.'

'And Donny?'

Devereux smiled sadly. 'They found Donny hanging in his cell the following night. He had made a rope by ripping his bed sheet into strips and plaiting them together.'

'But you helped him!'

'I did, but he had experienced a reality he could not adjust to: the prospect of five years looking over his shoulder; five years being the pretty one who would always draw the attention of predators; five years when I might not happen along. It was more than he could cope with. So he chose not to.'

I lit a cigarette. 'I'm sorry, Karl.'

'Mmm. So am I. But that day, when I went back to my cell, and was alone in the darkness, I pondered two things. After learning of Donny's suicide, I visited the three men who tried to rape him, and I hurt them – badly. Afterwards, Donny was no more alive than he had been beforehand. Revenge had achieved nothing, and I feared it had debased me as much as them. Secondly, I meditated upon my childhood, for the first time in many years. I followed the thread of occurrences that had brought that child to Mountjoy, and I began to realize that it might have happened differently, if someone had come upon me in a moment of dread. And somewhere in the early hours of a March morning, I made the decision to try and become that someone.'

He pushed back his stool and stood. 'I doubt that helps you much.'

'I genuinely don't know,' I said. 'But thanks, Karl.'

He nodded and was gone. I sat, alone again, and felt no better.

THEN

9

I was woken from sleep by a hand shaking me gently. I opened one eye and rolled over.

'Yeah?'

'I had an accthident,' Leo said. He hardly needed to tell me – I could smell the results of the mishap. I glanced at the fluorescent hands on my watch: 3.30 a.m.

'Okay, champ, let's go and get you cleaned up.'

I had been working at The Crow's Nest for two weeks, and I was not sure how much longer I could stick it. Jason's arrival had sent the other children into complete turmoil, and every shift had become a pitched battle between them and us. Leo's bowels, which teetered on the brink of disaster on a good day, now seemed to be seeping almost constantly, as a result of the stress he was under.

Jason was impossible to deal with at the best of times. After his assault on Yolanda, I had spent the next two hours holding him in a restraint on my knee, during which time he had wet himself (and consequently me), repeatedly attempted to bite whichever bit of my anatomy seemed nearest, and then projectile vomited at Ellen, who had responded by punching him so hard she gave him a black eye. The terrified girl had then rushed upstairs and locked herself in the shower. It had taken Terri an hour and a half to coax her out.

Jason learned from the experience, though, and made it his mission to try and smear Ellen with something disgusting every time he could get close enough to do so. Contamination was one of Ellen's most acute fears, and somehow, young as he was, Jason understood this, and used it against her mercilessly. Mucus from his nose, phlegm, faeces, earwax, or whatever he could find in the garden (fresh bird-droppings were a particular favourite) were all applied liberally. Ellen learned to run when she saw him coming. It would have been funny if she were not so genuinely terrified.

Mark also experienced severe problems around Jason, as the smaller boy worked out very quickly that his older cohort had a sensitivity to certain types of sound: high-pitched noises bothered him intensely, so Jason took to squealing every time Mark was within earshot. This would drive Mark into a frenzy, and he would have to be taken as far away from the source of the problem as possible.

It took me a couple of shifts to realize that this was all a scheme to earn our youngest house-guest plenty of one-to-one attention. It got so that Sarah and the other children would all spend the bulk of their time at the other end of the house, and he and I would spend most of the day together. Terri would move between both groups, but, as Sarah was dealing with the larger number of distressed children, she was the natural priority.

This left me emotionally and physically exhausted each evening. It was not that Jason was difficult to keep amused; in fact, he usually entertained himself. It was just that, regardless which toy, game, or piece of equipment he decided to play with, every play session was likely to end in violence. He would try to break the toy, use it to try and bludgeon me, or attempt to harm himself in some way.

Furthermore, the fact that his span of concentration lasted little more than ten minutes meant that I was on tenterhooks constantly. I did everything I could to try and extend his sport, but all to no effect. I would jabber away about whatever toy he was focused on, try to help him imagine the context of the game, suggest other ways of playing, and he would behave as if I was not there, until the truck was flung in the general direction of my head. This act would be accompanied by a raucous laugh, and then we would lapse back into silence.

I mused on this state of affairs as I followed the reeking Leo to the downstairs bathroom. 'You know the drill, kiddo,' I said. 'Leave the soiled clothes in the sink, and hop on into the shower. I'll get some fresh PJs and leave them on the radiator. Follow me up to your room when you're done, and you can help me make your bed.'

Bed-wetting and -soiling are commonplace in most residential settings, and no child is ever made to feel ashamed or embarrassed by the problem. The team had developed a policy that the children, if old enough, should take part in cleaning up the mess, though, so Leo knew to rinse out his clothes and leave them for the wash, and that he was expected to assist with putting clean sheets on his bed.

As I pulled linen from the airing cupboard, I heard steps on the stairs and, looking around the door, found Terri, wrapped in a dressing gown, padding towards me.

'Heard someone moving,' she yawned. 'Thought it might be the Red Lady.'

'Just me and Leo.'

'Exploding bowels?'

''Fraid so.'

'Fancy a cuppa before you go back to bed?'

'I'm awake now.'

'I'll put the kettle on.'

I got Leo settled, and joined Terri in the kitchen, where she had brewed a pot of camomile tea.

'How you finding it?' she asked, as I sipped the soothing brew.

'You weren't wrong,' I admitted. 'It's the toughest thing I've ever done.'

'You gonna run out on me?'

I grinned and shook my head. 'Not yet, blondie.'

She punched me gently on the shoulder. 'Good. I think Jason kind of likes you.'

I laughed aloud. 'You're not serious. I'm only good for target practice!'

'Would he work so hard to keep everyone else away if he didn't want you all to himself?'

'He wants to keep us all separate so he can fuck me around without distraction.'

'I think there's more to it than that. Mark my words.'

Terri finished her tea, rinsed her mug out in the sink and went back to bed. I sat a while longer and smoked a cigarette, then did a quick check of the rooms, to make sure everyone was where they were supposed to be – bed-hopping could be a problem, and where so many of the children had been sexually abused, this was not something we wanted to encourage.

Everyone was present and correct until I came to Jason's room. The bed was empty, and the door wide open. I stood for a second, feeling vexed and slightly panicked all at the same time. This was the last thing I wanted to deal with. If I didn't find him quickly, it would mean waking Terri and Sarah, and doing a full-scale search of the house. I was fairly confident he had not managed to get outside, as all the doors and windows were locked, but I did not underestimate his resourcefulness, and knew that dawn might well find me clambering through shrubs in the garden.

I was about to open Jason's wardrobe to see if he might be hiding in there when I heard a whimper. It was almost inaudible, and had I been moving, the sound of my footsteps, soft as they were in the middle of the night, would have caused me to miss it. I stood very still and stopped breathing, and, in a moment, there it was again. Someone was crying softly, and a short exploration of the room proved the sounds were coming from under the bed.

I squatted down on my haunches, remaining close to the door, and peered into the gloom. I could just make out a figure pressed up against the skirting board. As I watched, I was able to discern the glint of eyes.

'Hey, Jason,' I said gently. 'What are you doing under there?'

The sobbing continued.

'Did you have a bad dream?'

Still no answer other than muffled weeping. Slowly, painfully, still on my toes, I edged closer.

'It must be scary for you, in this big old house with a lot of strange people. I bet you miss your mum and dad, your big brother. Your toys too, I'd say. It's been a really tough few weeks, hasn't it?'

Those dark eyes watched me immutably as I reached the side of the bed. I saw that the child had rolled himself into a foetal position, his arms wrapped about his knees. I knew it was common for children who had experienced sexual abuse to sleep under the bed rather than in it, a pathetic attempt to protect themselves from the horrors that may find them during the hours of darkness. I

75

reasoned that Jason had either had a nightmare, or heard me moving about the house, and terrified himself by imagining ill intent behind such nocturnal travels.

'I just came to check on you, to see if you were okay,' I said. 'I'm not going to hurt you.'

The boy was shaking. I didn't know if it was from nerves or the cold.

'Jason, you can stay under there, if you like,' I said. 'Or you can come out and get back into bed. I don't mind one way or the other, but if you want to stay where you are, I think you might be more comfortable if I passed a blanket in to you. What do you say?'

The bitter tears had all but abated, and those eyes watched me, unblinking. I wasn't sure what to do. I pulled a blanket from the bed and folded it loosely. I pushed it a little way towards Jason, not wanting to frighten him any more than he already was by getting too close. 'D'you want to take this, Jase? You'll be warmer.'

He made no move towards it, just remained hunched into his corner, a ball of pain and tension.

I sighed and sat down on the floor – my legs were getting stiff.

'Want to come out?'

Still nothing. I tentatively reached my arm out. Did I see the tiniest fraction of movement? I left my arm there, my fingers all straining for the boy. Slowly, as if his small limbs were unused to the action, Jason began to move his arm in my direction. I held my breath and didn't move. It seemed to take forever, but then, in one burst of movement, he sprang across the floor and grabbed my wrist. I hauled him out, and attempted to bundle him on to the bed. Except he would not let go of me. I stood for a minute, uncertain of what to do next. Jason's skinny arms

76

were wrapped around my neck tightly, and his knees dug into my ribs. I sat down slowly on the edge of the bed, not wanting to make any sudden movements, and just held him. He was still trembling, and I realized that he was all goosebumps. I rocked him gently, and sang him a lullaby, and in time I sensed him relax, and his breath grew deep and steady, and then he was asleep.

I laid him on the mattress and pulled the quilt over him, then walked back downstairs. The rising sun found me sitting on the front doorstep smoking, and trying to make sense of what had just happened. It proved a futile exercise. I was no wiser when Sarah found me there two hours later.

10

Jason met me at breakfast with stony, indignant silence, and he ate his cereal with his usual reckless disregard for the niceties of etiquette. The other children always hurried their meals in a bid to keep Jason at a distance, and soon enough it was just him and me in the kitchen. I poured myself another cup of coffee, and watched him shove an entire slice of toast into his mouth in one go.

'I can tell you're kind of mad at me this morning,' I said. 'That's okay. But you don't need to be embarrassed about being scared in the night. Everyone here has been scared at one time or another. We try to help one another with things like that, here. That's what friends do.'

Jason slurped from his glass of milk, and farted like a foghorn.

'Did you have any friends before you came here, Jase?' I asked. I continually tried to treat him as if he was a real chatterbox. I refused to facilitate his mutism by compensating in any way. He would often point at something, waiting for me to pass it to him, or in the case of food to prepare it, but I would simply look at him blankly. 'What do you want?' I'd ask. 'You have to tell me.'

This would usually be greeted by angry hoots and growls, until he got up in frustration and got the desired item and handed it to me. I treated our chats just the same way. I would ask him questions, and refuse to move on with the conversation until I had received some kind of response. This might involve Jason storming off, bellowing at me wordlessly, or, if I was really lucky and he was in something of a good mood (or as close as my young charge ever got to such a pleasant frame of mind), a shake or nod of the head. That morning, I knew I would not be in for an easy ride. Any interaction would be hard won, but I had another six hours before my shift was over, and I figured I might as well try and capitalize on the breakthrough of the night before.

'Did you ever go to school, Jason, or play on the street? Did you have any favourite games?'

The boy pushed back his chair abruptly, walked over to the patio door, and went into the garden. I followed. 'Did you have a best friend, Jason? It's nice to have a buddy you can share things with, isn't it?'

It was a beautiful morning, and the sun was already warm on my back as I tailed Jason to the front of the house. The cawing of the crows, an almost constant background to all my time in The Crow's Nest, seemed gentle and hypnotic. Jason made for the gate, and, as there was no traffic on the road, I allowed him to cross without intervening. A shaded pathway wound through the trees and lawns to a small playground, complete with a slide, a set of swings, a sandpit, a seesaw and a roundabout. It was there that Jason was making for. I had been with him several times before, but when the other children were present, playing boisterously on the amusements, he tended to become morose and ill at ease, and usually did not remain for long. As early in the day as it was, the boy seemed confident that he would have the area to himself, and he was right.

He sat on one of the swings that was lower to the ground, and better suited to his height, and simply perched there, the wind blowing his straggly hair, and an expression almost of peace on his face. I stopped trying to coax some words from him, and drew back. I sensed that, maybe for the first time since coming to us, Jason was happy. I didn't want to ruin it.

We stayed for more than an hour, and the boy spent most of that time sitting on that swing, dangling his legs, sometimes leaning back a little to make it sway in the gentle breeze, seemingly in a kind of rapture. At one point, he wandered aimlessly over to the slide, and climbed up one or two rungs on the ladder, but he stopped then, apparently unsure how to proceed, and carefully went back down. I watched him do that several times, until realization dawned: he was afraid.

It occurred to me that Jason had probably never been taken to the park, and therefore had no concept of how all the installations worked. He knew it was meant to be fun, and was clearly responding to all the primary colours of the paintwork, and being out of doors, but he had always been so antagonistic and territorial with the other children during previous visits that he had probably paid little attention to what everyone had been doing. I watched as he climbed up and down off the roundabout, but made no effort to spin it, and had my suspicions confirmed. I waited for him to step off again, and then went over and gave the contraption two or three strong kicks, setting it whirring around. 'Jason, look at me!' I said as I leaped on to the roundabout. The little boy stood there, his mouth hanging open, as I whooshed past him. I used my boot as a break, and came to a juddering halt. 'Want to get on?' There was no pause this time: a very definite nod was the answer. 'Come on, then.'

He came over in stuttering steps, and held on tightly to the bar with one hand, and my trouser leg with the other.

'You ready?' Another nod, this one accompanied by a nervous grin. 'Okay, and – we're off!'

I kicked gently, this time, and we began to turn slowly. Jason squealed and laughed in delight, bouncing on the balls of his feet in joy. I didn't make the roundabout go much faster, but we stayed on for a good twenty minutes, until I was thoroughly nauseous, but I dared not call an end to Jason's undisguised pleasure. When he was done, he jogged over to the swing, sat down, and looked at me expectantly. I remained by the roundabout.

'Would you like me to show you how the swings work?'

Again a clear affirmative. I sat on the swing next to him, and leaned well back, kicked forward, and set the seat shooting back and forth.

'Ooohhh!' Jason said in wonder.

I got off and stood behind him. 'Will I help you do that?'

He leaned back so he could see me. Nod.

'Okay.' I pulled his swing back, and pushed him off. 'Kick with your legs,' I said. 'You'll go that bit higher.'

From the swings we went to the seesaw and from there to the slide. Once again, I demonstrated the trick for him, but this time my display was met with a look of fear and discomfort. 'You don't like this one?'

He shook his head: no.

'Would you like to go up with me right behind, so you don't fall, and then you can slide down on my knee?'

Another no.

I stood and looked at the slide. It wasn't a particularly high one, but to Jason, who was so small and inexperienced in such things, it must have appeared huge, indeed.

'Want to go on the seesaw again?' I asked.

Grinning from ear to ear, Jason virtually skipped over. Beaming like a child on his birthday, I followed. The slide could wait for another day.

11

Jason sat on the floor of the consultant's office, looking at the pictures in a comic book. The medic, Mr Ledwidge Harbison, was telling Terri and me there was nothing physically wrong with the boy, and that his lack of verbal communication was down to psychological reasons. We had driven to Belfast to see him, and it was looking like a wasted journey.

'He's small for his age,' Mr Harbison said evenly, 'and shows some fine-motor retardation, but, other than that, I can see nothing wrong with him. He has a voice box, and is well able to vocalize. He's just not using language.'

I smiled politely, and tried to pretend that he had not just told me what I already knew. Terri was not so cooperative.

'Doc, we haven't come all this way for you to send us away no better than we were before drivin' more than two hundred miles on crappy roads with a hyperactive five-year-old. Can he speak or not?'

'He understands language, that much is obvious,' Harbison said, realizing that he was not going to be able to bluff his way past this blonde amazon, 'and you inform me that his family report that he spoke before being taken into care.'

'They're not what I'd call reliable witnesses,' Terri said drily.

'Why not?' Harbison asked.

'They tortured the kid, and are getting prosecuted for

it. Anything they say has to be taken in the context of looking for a more lenient sentence,' Terri responded.

'Oh.'

'Mr Harbison,' I asked, my patience running thin, 'can you give us a definitive answer, or are we dealing with one of those "not an exact science" sort of things?'

Harbison looked uncomfortable. 'My professional opinion is that Jason Farrell can certainly speak, but chooses not to, probably due to the traumatic experience of being removed from his family.'

'But we'll just have to wait and see,' Terri finished.

'Yes.'

We said little on the drive home. Thankfully, Jason slept most of the way.

12

Friday night was video night. It was something we all looked forward to, as it was an excuse to raid the junk-food cupboard (every residential unit has one – the value of chocolate to the overall sense of emotional wellbeing of a child can never be overstated), and the children were allowed to stay up late. We would descend upon the local video rental shop (DVDs were still some years away) and the children would pick something. We usually let them have a pretty free rein on what they wanted and, in fairness to them, they tended towards pretty harmless family-oriented stuff. To my disgust, the ex-hibited a great love for musicals, and I was forced to sit through *Grease*, *Oklahoma!* and *Calamity Jane* over my first three video evenings. My fourth Friday offered no respite. Leo presented me with a copy of Lionel Bart's *Oliver!*.

'Conthider yourthelf a lucky fella!' he said. 'Thith ith a good one!'

'That's a matter of opinion, Leo,' I said, paying for the tape.

'A clathic ith a clathic,' Leo said, feigning offence. 'Look at the catht litht.'

'You're too young to know who Oliver Reed is!' I said. 'Now come on. The longer we spend debating the relative merits of the movie, the less popcorn there'll be. Sarah will have eaten it all.'

'Home, Shane, and don't thpare the hortheth!' Leo said, making for the car.

Leo, Mark and Ellen had all seen *Oliver!* before. I was learning that video night tended to involve the kids renting out the same movies repeatedly. It was, however, a new experience for Jason, who sat on the floor, almost on top of the screen, his dark eyes wide as the story of abandonment, redemption and triumph played out – along with many show tunes. I must admit, I did find myself enjoying Ron Moody's roguish Fagin, and Jack Wilde was irresistible as the Artful Dodger. I'm a fan of Dickens, and was acutely aware that the darker elements of the story were very much toned down for the musical, but the children nevertheless understood very clearly that Oliver Twist was alone in the world, that the poorhouse was where they would all have been had they lived a hundred years earlier. And I got the impression they had all had experience of Bill Sykes, in one form or other.

When the credits were rolling, I stood up stiffly and began to gather up the empty bowls and candy wrappers.

'All right, you lot. Brush your teeth and off to bed.'

Jason didn't move. He was pointing at the video recorder, and making an urgent grunting sound.

'D'you want to see the film again, Jason?' Sarah asked.

Jason nodded, and banged the floor with his heels.

'Come on, it's bedtime, now. Too late,' Sarah laughed. 'You can see it again tomorrow.'

'He liked it, didn't he?' Mark said as he got up from the couch. 'That's because he's like Oliver. No one wants him.'

'Um, Mithter Brownlow wanted Oliver,' Leo interceded. 'And Bill Thykes kind of wanted him, too, although hith motives were questionable . . .'

'Shut up, Leo. You never had any parents to begin with, so you don't know!' Mark said.

'I didn't gethtate in that shoe boxth, you know!' Leo said, glaring at Mark.

'I'm not talking about you, anyway,' Mark snapped. 'I'm talking about that little scumbag.'

'Hey, that's not kind,' I said. 'If you can't be nice, keep your opinions to yourself, Mark.'

'It's true,' Ellen pitched in. 'We don't like him, and I heard that his parents used to lock him away so they didn't have to look at him. His mum and dad hated him, so they did.'

Jason's grunting had stopped during this exchange, but as Ellen articulated this final insult, he let loose a howl and launched himself at her, his hands bared like claws. I managed to intercept him, and caught him under my arm, swinging him away from Ellen.

'Go on, you nasty little boy,' Ellen spat. 'I'm not surprised your parents didn't want you. I wouldn't be surprised if you never see them again.'

'That's it, young lady,' Sarah said, leading her from the room. 'You owe Jason an apology, but right now, I want you to go straight to your room. You both need to calm down.'

Mark and Leo had already made themselves scarce, and I held the snarling, struggling Jason until he wore himself out. This time his anger dissipated into grief, and he cried piteously, leaning into my shoulder and holding on to my arms with a vice-like grip. I shushed him, and stroked his hair, and waited for the crying to cease. Finally it did, and he lay against me, hiccuping and sighing deeply, as if his troubles were so great, he had lost all will to continue fighting them. I was about to carry him to the bathroom to wash his face, when a hoarse little voice said: 'Shane?'

He sounded like speaking was an effort, and I supposed that four weeks of inarticulacy might cause that.

'Yes, Jason,' I answered, not wanting to behave as if his suddenly deciding to talk was anything unusual.

'Will my mammy be coming back for me?'

I hugged him tightly to me, and felt tears rising in my own eyes. Such a simple question, yet such an incredibly loaded one.

'I don't know, Jason,' I admitted. I couldn't lie to him.

'Don't she love me no more, Shane?'

'Of course she does,' I said, the tears audible in my voice, now. I didn't care. This bereft little boy deserved to have someone cry for him. 'You must never forget that. She loves you very much.'

'Where is she, then?' he asked, his tiny, gravelly voice close to my ear. 'They tooked me, and I haven't seen her or my dad or my brudder. I'm scared they don't know where I am. How can they come and get me if they don't know where I am?'

I pulled him away from my shoulder and looked at him. His funny, little old man's face was wan with exhaustion and grief. 'They know you're here, and they want to see you, and we can make sure they do, okay?'

'Promise me? A real, big promise, one what you can't break, no matter what?'

'Yes,' I laughed, tears still streaming down my face. 'I promise – just like that.'

'When?'

'That's hard, Jason. That's a hard one for me to say.

88

But I will talk to the social workers and see if I can set something up tomorrow, okay?'

'Not Yolanda, though.'

'No. Yolanda doesn't work with you any more.'

'Cause o' what I done?'

I nodded.

'I think I'd like to go to bed now.'

'Okay.'

'Will you stay with me until I falls asleep?'

I nodded again.

Sarah met us at the door and, reaching over, kissed us both on our foreheads. '*Well done*,' she whispered in my ear.

13

Jason's speech did not come back in the great gush I had hoped it would when words finally returned to him. Rather they seeped back into his life slowly, uneasily, as if by articulating what he was feeling, the child was leaving himself vulnerable to attack or further abuse.

One morning, two days after we had watched *Oliver!*, I went into the kitchen to get myself a cup of coffee. There, peering into one of the kitchen cupboards, was Jason. So engrossed was he in his vigil, he did not notice my presence. I stopped and watched him for a moment, trying to work out what so captivated him in the press.

'What are you looking at, Jase?' I finally ventured.

'Shane,' he said, in hushed tones, 'this cupboard is magic.'

This was my first acquaintance with the enchanted storage unit. I had heard of the Red Lady, our house ghost; Ellen had assured me that the crows could send thought waves at us and were planning an attack; and Leo sometimes appeared to be from another planet. But a magic cupboard was definitely a new one on me.

'Is it?' I asked. 'How?'

'When I had breakfast this morning,' Jason said, 'all the cornflakes were gone. Now look' – he produced a brand-new, unopened box – 'these are here!'

I didn't know whether to laugh or cry. In this child's previous experience, in a home where such things as the basic staples were considered a luxury, when the cornflakes were finished, it could be months before they were replenished. For another box to appear so quickly had to be magic.

I looked at the little boy: underweight even after several months in care, his clean new clothes still too big for him, his face lit up with joy at the prospect of a full box of breakfast cereal. I went over and hugged him. The fact that Sarah had picked up that box of cornflakes, along with a boot-load of other groceries several hours earlier, seemed unimportant. If Jason thought it was magic, then I was prepared to believe him.

Jason's new social worker was a young man named Fionn Jackson. I had to call the Health Board offices three times to find out this information, as, in the four weeks since Yolanda had resigned from her post, he had not once made contact with either the boy, or us, his carers.

He met me for lunch in a small café by the river. I was twenty years old, but he looked younger. He seemed nervous and jumpy, and I wondered if his career choice was suiting him.

'You're asking me if we can organize access visits between Jason Farrell and his parents?'

'There's an older brother, too.'

'Oh, right. Paddy, isn't it?'

'Timmy.'

'Of course, yes . . .' He had the almost empty file open on the table in front of him. 'Um . . . there seems to be a history of fairly severe abuse here. Are you sure access would be wise?'

'Jason was taken into care several months ago. He has neither seen nor heard from any member of his family during that time. You know how kids in care can have serious abandonment issues?'

'Well of course.'

'Jason's is being made a hell of a lot worse because no one has even told him how his family is doing. He's devastated.'

'I see. Access would have to be fully supervised.'

'That's fine. Just let this child see his family – please.'

We said nothing for a time as we applied ourselves to our respective sandwiches.

'Is he still violent?' Fionn asked, then. He was a slim, blond-haired, delicate-looking youngster.

'Yes. Very violent, sometimes.'

'But you say he is speaking now?'

'Started two days ago. It's not much, and it's primarily to me, but he's communicating, yes.'

Fionn sipped his tea and mopped his lips with a serviette. 'Does he speak about his home life at all? What we have is very sketchy, but it would appear his family, including this older sibling, were horrifically unpleasant towards him. It would be good to know more. Do you think you might get him talking about it?'

In a few years' time, I would have seen this request for what it was, but at this early stage in my career, with little experience to fall back on, I took it at face value. I was flattered: I had made a breakthrough on a difficult case, and here was a social worker, my superior, to all intents and purposes, asking me to try and move the case forward even more. The fact that the information would be needed for the pending prosecution of Jason's parents, and that I would be getting the child to cement his parents' ruin, never once occurred to me.

'I'll see what I can do,' I said.

'That would be marvellous. If there's anything you need, why not give me a call? I'd be happy to help in any way I can.'

'There is one thing I need, actually,' I said.

'And what's that?'

He looked surprised when I told him, but wrote out a requisition slip for it straight away. Over the next ten months, he would visit The Crow's Nest three times, and two of those occasions were during the trial. In his own way, though, he helped Jason, not least by signing off on my guitar.

14

I owned a couple of guitars, but there was no way I was going to bring either of them into work. There wasn't an item in the playroom that hadn't been wrecked (mostly by Jason, but the other three kids were not beyond kicking or throwing toys and games when irritated by something), so there was no way any of my precious instruments were going to be brought into that war zone.

Yet I felt, particularly after sitting through all those musicals and listening to the kids singing along so enthusiastically to the various set pieces (and since he'd found his voice I had even heard Jason croaking the chorus of 'You've Got to Pick a Pocket or Two' when he thought no one was listening), that bringing some music into the house might be a positive thing.

The guitar I bought was a second-hand Fender steel-stringed acoustic. The man in the shop informed me that it was a 1960s model, but I wasn't sure I believed him, particularly at the price he was asking, which was considerably less than Fionn had signed off on. The guitar had a lovely tone, though, and looked so battered I didn't feel the children would see much point in heaping abuse on it. I bought a few spare sets of strings, some plectrums and an even more decrepit-looking case, and I was set.

On my next shift, I carried the old guitar in with great ceremony, and the children all gathered round, eyes wide.

'Stand back now,' I said. 'Everyone can get a look and have a go, but if there's any rough play, I'll put it away and you won't see it for the rest of the day. Are we clear?'

There was general agreement, and the guitar was passed around reasonably fairly. As I had suspected, when none of them could get much more than a discordant clanging from the instrument, it was returned to me.

'Play thomething we can thing along to,' Leo said. 'Thomething happy.'

That, to my surprise, stumped me for a moment. As a young musician, I tended more towards maudlin, navel-gazing pieces, and had to think really hard before I could even call to mind a song that was both suitable for young ears, and met the criteria of being happy. Finally, I settled upon one of Woody Guthrie's children's songs, 'Drivin' in My Car'. It's a simple, chorus-driven piece, and the group picked it up immediately, and joined in enthusiastically.

> *I'll take you drivin' in my car, boys,*
> *I'll take you drivin' in my car.*
> *Let's go drivin' in my car, girls,*
> *We'll go drivin' in my car.*

Each verse focused on a different aspect of the experience, and had its own sound effects and actions:

> *Listen to the horn go* beep! Beep!

or

> *The engine it goes* boom! Boom!

Everyone took turns making up verses, then, with all sorts of imaginative additions to the list of things on a car that could make noises – doors went squeak, tyres burst loudly as they punctured, puddles went splash as we drove through them – the short song turned into a fifteen-minute epic, and we all had a grand old time. I was applauded roundly, and made no secret of the fact that I felt I deserved all the praise my audience could heap upon me.

'Yes, I am very talented. More clapping, please. I'm worth it.'

'We'd better thtop, before hith head getth tho big, he won't fit out the front door any more,' Leo said, grinning.

'Would anyone else like to sing something for us?' Sarah suggested. 'I'm sure you all have favourite songs.'

'I can do Elvis,' Mark said, blushing slightly.

'Oooh, let's hear it, then,' Sarah said, and Mark self-consciously stood up and, in a perfect Memphis drawl, began to sing – and dance. The sight of a young man with fairly severe dyspraxia – often called 'the clumsy syndrome' – trying to replicate the King's snake-hipped movements was something to behold. I played along (it was actually a Buddy Holly song Mark chose to sing – 'Oh Boy'), trying desperately not to laugh, but the children were not in the least bothered by Mark's bizarre movements and complete lack of grace. They cheered and encouraged, even Jason, who seemed to be beside himself with joy at the whole exercise. Mark's performance was rewarded by an even greater round of applause than my car song, which I pretended to be a bit miffed at.

'You're beating Shane on the clapometer, I think, Mark,' Sarah said, winking at me. 'Who's next?'

'I'd like to thing, pleathe,' Leo said.

'Off you go, then.'

This time, the laughter could not be repressed. With a completely deadpan expression, and not leaving out a single one of the actions, Leo treated us to 'I'm a Little Teapot'. By the time he was halfway through the song, Leo realized he was on to a winner, and hammed up a second refrain of it dreadfully, but there was not a dry eye in the house when he had finished.

'Thanks you, ladieth and gentlemen, I'll be playing here all week,' he said, blowing kisses at us all as he went back to his seat.

'Would you like to sing something, Ellen?' I asked.

She nodded.

'What would you like to do for us?'

'A song my mammy taught me.'

'Okay, love. In your own time,' I said.

What happened next is one of those occurrences that I always put down to the remarkable power of music. I've seen it time and again, but it never fails to stop me in my tracks, nonetheless. Ellen remained seated, but she closed her eyes, and began to sing, softly, but very sweetly, and note-perfect. The song was an old ballad, and could be seen as something of a cliché for a child in her situation, but that morning, all any of us heard was the truth in the words. It was, simply, very moving.

I was slowly passing an orphans' home one day
And stopped there for a moment just to watch the children play.
Alone a girl was standing and when I asked her why
She turned with eyes that could not see and she began to cry.

'People come for children and take them for their own.
But they all seem to pass me by and I am left alone.
I know they'd like to take me but when they see I'm blind
They always take some other child and I am left behind.

No mother's arms to hold me or soothe me when I cry.
Sometimes it gets so lonely I wish that I could die.
I'd walk the streets of heaven where all the blind can see.
And just like all the other kids there'd be a home for me.

I'm nobody's child; nobody's child.
I'm like a flower just growing wild.
No mommy's kisses, and no daddy's smile.
Nobody wants me, I'm nobody's child.'

There was little I could do to back her on the guitar – I just found the key she was singing in, and strummed on the beat, behind her. When she was finished, she opened her eyes, and smiled a nervous smile. We were all clapping and telling her how beautifully she had sung, when, without warning, Jason got up from his chair, went over to Ellen, and – he had to climb on to the couch to do it – hugged her. Too amazed to say anything, Ellen simply accepted the gesture. Sarah and I exchanged surreptitious glances. Jason held the girl tightly, and in his odd, gruff way, said: 'We want you, Ellen.' He planted a wet kiss on her cheek, tousled her hair, and then went back to his seat beside me. Ellen seemed genuinely overcome by the experience, but, not wanting to draw too much attention to it, I struck up a riff quickly. 'Come on, Leo,' I said. 'Let's hear some of those show tunes you love so much.'

All the while Jason sat there, a gentle smile on his face, joining in with the songs every now and again, seemingly oblivious to the remarkable change he had gone through.

NOW

15

The Farrells lived in a crumbling local-authority house in the middle of a huge housing estate. I rode the bus out, and walked in the rain through the maze of streets and identical houses until I found their abode. The porch had long ago been taken over by spiders who had woven webs across every corner. These were now beaded by raindrops and looked almost pretty in the grey light. A car that did not look as if it had been driven in a very long time sat in the driveway, moss growing luxuriantly on the roof. I knocked loudly. It was eleven thirty in the morning, but I was still not certain that anyone would be up and about. Finally, I heard footsteps approaching, and a figure appeared silhouetted in the glass panel beside the door.

'Hello, Mrs Farrell,' I said when the door opened a crack. 'My name is Shane Dunphy. I don't know if you remember me from the time Jason was at The Crow's Nest? I was his key-worker.'

The woman squinted. She was tall and thin, her dark hair lank and unwashed. She wore a floral dressing gown, and her skinny legs were bare beneath it.

'Oh – yeah, sure. You look a lot older.'

'It's been eleven years, Mrs Farrell. We're all a lot older.'

'Jason's not here.'

'I know. He's in St Phelim's. I took him there.'

'What do you want, then?'

'To talk, for a moment. It's fairly wet out here, Mrs Farrell. Can I step inside?'

'The house isn't tidy.'

'That's fine. I'm not very tidy myself.'

She stood aside, and I went in. The house smelled of cooking fat and cigarette smoke. I didn't care. It was dry. She brought me into a sparsely decorated living room. There were two armchairs, a small oddment (it looked like a narrow spindly table, but it would have held little more than a single coffee cup) upon which an overflowing ashtray sat, and a huge flat-screen television with massive speakers, which took over one side of the room. Jeremy Kyle was playing with the sound muted. A woman, who looked not unlike Jason's mother, was speaking urgently to the dour host. I turned away. Jeremy Kyle always depressed me. There was something cynical about the show that left a bad taste in my mouth.

Mrs Farrell took a pack of cigarettes from the pocket of her dressing gown and lit one. I followed her lead.

'What do you want, mister?' she said. 'Jason got himself in trouble, and there's nothin' I can do for him, now. He's always been trouble, ever since he were a little lad. Sure, you remember that. You knew him when he was small. He was a bad one, even then.'

'He was five years old, Mrs Farrell. A child of that age can't be bad. They can be messed up and angry and mixed up about who they are, but they are most certainly not bad.'

'Well, pardon me for breathin',' the woman said, obviously warming to her subject. 'As far as I'm concerned, Jason can keep away this time. He came here a year ago, lookin' to move back in. Said he wanted to start again, try to get a job, make somethin' of hisself. Now, he's my flesh and blood, so I said I'd give him a chance, not that he deserved it after what he put me through, but I said okay, against my better judgement. Well, it was just one thing after another. The guards were always knockin' on my door about him. And it wasn't all robbin' stuff, neither. They said he was interferin' with kids. I mean, that's an awful carry on. We never done that here.'

'You have a short memory, Mrs Farrell,' I said.

She ignored me.

'I caught him with drugs one time. I got mad, and I hit him. I think that's where we went wrong with him, really. He wasn't slapped enough. He never had any respect.'

I bit my tongue. The desire to remind her of the reasons her son had been in care in the first place were almost overpowering. But I needed this awful woman. I had to keep her on side.

'Mrs Farrell, is your husband about?'

'Conor? No, he's long gone. Couldn't stick it around here any more, and I don't blame him. Should have gone myself. It's just, well, I grew up in the Oldtown, been here all my life. Don't know no place else.'

'I understand. What about Timmy?'

'Gone.'

'So it's just you?'

'My brothers come around sometimes.'

'It's just that Phelim's are talking about putting Jason on a programme, one that will help him to stop doing all the bad stuff he does. But see, he needs support, for when he gets out. And the people who are going to be there for him, they need to be involved in the programme, too. Without them, he can't participate in it. Would you do that for him?'

'I'm finished with Jason, so I am. He's not a good boy.'

'He could be.'

'No. Why would I? Why would I go to that trouble for him?'

I gripped the arm of the chair. This was not going as I had planned. 'He's your son.'

'No. No son of mine.'

I sighed deeply, and played my trump card. After this, I had nothing, and Jason could expect a lengthy custodial sentence.

'Mrs Farrell, they'd pay you.'

A smile spread across her swarthy face. 'Sure maybe we could talk about it, at least. It can't hurt none, now can it?'

16

'Timmy Farrell shot himself in the head with a nine-millimetre Glock hand-gun just under a year ago,' Rachel Keane said. She ran the community centre closest to the Farrells' home. We were sitting in her office drinking coffee. 'He was a pretty messed-up young man. Not bad, just sad.'

Rachel was in her early thirties, plump and smiling, and spoke with a West of Ireland accent.

'Where you from?'

'Connemara.'

'You're a long way from home.'

'It's not all that different.'

'Did you know Jason?'

'Some. He came home just before Timmy died. He was way crazier than his older brother. There was a kind of meanness there. I've been told that he was a pederast, that he wasn't safe around little children. From what I saw, no one was safe around him. He came in here once, looking for me to give him money. When he saw that he genuinely wasn't going to get any, well, his tone changed immediately.'

'How? What was the difference?'

'Before, he'd been sort of trying to be charming. He wasn't, not by a long shot, but he was doing his best impression of it, if you know what I mean. But when I got firm, and really put my foot down, he just, well, it was as if someone had hit a switch and he was a different person.

Those dark, black eyes of his flashed, and he told me that if he couldn't get anything out of me one way, he'd get it another. He tried to push my desk so that I was pinned to the wall. It was sort of pathetic, because he's such a little thing, he didn't have the strength to do it. In that time, I'd hit the alarm button on my phone, we all have them –'

'With good reason,' I said.

'Well, precisely. He tried to jump across the desk and grab me, but two of the other support workers, two big guys, had come in by then, and he was thrown out.'

I cradled my coffee cup in my two hands, using it for warmth as much as anything else. 'Do you think he would have raped you if he'd had the chance?'

'There is no doubt in my mind whatsoever.'

'I was afraid you'd say that,' I said. 'What about his mother?'

'Liz Farrell? She's an alcoholic and she doesn't seem to care about those kids. She put on a show when Timmy committed suicide, but I mean to say, questions have to be asked about why that boy took a gun to himself in the first place. I don't like the term "poor white trash", but in a lot of ways, that's what this family is, and I'd guess there's generations of abuse and neglect, and maybe even worse, on both sides.'

'More than likely,' I agreed. 'But tell me – Mr Farrell – he's done a bunk?'

'Apparently,' Rachel said. 'He was never exactly a shining beacon of hope and humanity. No great loss.'

'But he was the real figurehead of the family as I remember him,' I said. 'It seems odd that he'd take off.'

'Maybe Liz just got too difficult to live with. Then again, he might owe someone money, or he might have pissed off one of the local heavies enough to have to lie low for a while – the possibilities are endless, Shane. It's all a part of life's rich pageant.'

'Did Jason have any friends you're aware of? Anyone he particularly hung out with, had a relationship with?'

'The closest relationship he had would have been with Timmy. Before he died they were very, very tight. Jason took it exceptionally badly when Timmy took his life. Other than that, there's the Quinns. But I'd hardly call them friends. It's more like he works for them.'

'They're the local hoods?'

'They're sort of middle-management in the Topsy Roberts gang. Their sister, Maisie, is married into the Roberts, so that gave them an in, although they're as thick as a plank, and not really very tough. They tend to be given things to do that they can't mess up. Jason used to hang out with them a little, but I think they spent most of their time smoking dope and telling each other lies about their exploits. There wasn't a lot of depth to their relationship, if you get my meaning.'

I finished my coffee and left the cup sitting on her desk.

'Does it ever get to you?' I asked.

'What?'

'I dunno – the hopelessness of it all.'

Rachel laughed. 'It's not all hopeless. There are some really good people out there. I've seen more of a sense of community here in the Oldtown than I've ever seen in the most picturesque little villages in Galway, where the lawns are all nicely mowed and the people all own four-wheel drives. I see lots of hope here, Shane. You've just caught a really tough one, is all.'

'Think he can be put right?'

Rachel pursed her lips. 'I don't believe in bad kids,' she

said. 'In our line of work, it doesn't help to think like that. But I don't believe in miracles, either.'

'And you think Jason might be in need of a miracle?'

She sat back and put her feet up on her desk. She was wearing new Doc Marten boots. 'My dad is a vet. When I was growing up, he'd often let me help him with some of the procedures. Nothing heavy – I'd pass him the instruments and look after the animals afterwards, stuff like that. I loved being with him, and I loved animals – still do – so it was a perfect arrangement.'

'Sounds ideal.'

'It was. Guess what my favourite animal is.'

'Fluffy bunny rabbit?'

'No, dumb-ass. The cow. I always loved cows.'

'I think the collective term is "cattle".'

She ignored me. 'One evening, my dad was called to a local farmer, because one of his cows had escaped on to the road and been hit by a truck. She was in bits, all torn up, outside and in, but somehow she was still alive. That farmer called my dad to have her put down, but my mum was out shopping, and it was too short notice to get a sitter, so he had to bring me along. I wasn't put off by the blood or the guts – I'd seen all that before – what upset me was the idea that my daddy was going to kill that poor cow.'

'Surely you'd seen him euthanize animals before?'

'No. He never let me see that. Well, I went ballistic. I roared and cried, and I begged him to save her. He explained that it was a kindness he was doing, but I'd have none of it. I lay down on the animal's side, and I wouldn't get up. The farmer must have had more money than sense, because he told my dad to see if he could patch her up. I remember my father telling him that it would take a miracle, that she was too badly damaged, but he tried anyway. He worked all through the night, and I stayed with him.'

The rain beat like tiny fists on the window, and a wind blew up from the south. It was warm and friendly in Rachel's office. We had just met, and were from different parts of the country. She was younger than me by at least five years, and we worked in different disciplines, but we knew one another, for all that.

'Did the cow live?' I asked.

'No,' Rachel said sadly. 'Dad was right, she was hurt too badly. But he tried, because I asked him to. And the animal deserved that chance – I still believe that. But see, in his heart, he knew she was done for. Sometimes, the hurt goes too deep.'

'But you have to try,' I said, vocalizing the moral of her story.

'Sometimes, that's all you can do,' Rachel said.

17

I bought Jason some clothes – mostly tracksuits and sports tops – and went over to Phelim's. I was starting to miss my Austin terribly. I didn't feel whole, somehow, without it, and determined to drop by the garage on the way home to check on its progress.

Jason was delighted with the outfits, and I had also thrown in some chocolate and comics. 'You always got me comics, didn'tcha?' he said.

'I like comics.'

'Yeah, I remember.'

I sat on the bed in his room, and watched as he folded the clothes carefully and put them in his chest of drawers. He was surprisingly meticulous.

'Tell me about you and Timmy,' I said.

'He was a sad fuckin' loser, is all I have to say about him,' Jason said. 'He let them beat him. He was weak.'

'Not like you.'

'No. Look at me. I been through shite, but I'm still standin'.'

'A tough guy.'

'Ya have to be.'

'I heard you and him were pretty tight.'

'Ah, maybe. Maybe before.'

'Timmy was ten years older than you.'

'So.'

'He was blamed for a lot of stuff that happened to you when you were little.'

'Ah, don't dredge all that shite up again,' Jason said irritably. 'That's long gone. I lives in the now.'

'So "the now" has you running around, threatening people, trying to entice children off to abuse them, and attacking old women, does it?'

Jason spun on me. 'Watch what you say. You got no right to talk to me like that.'

'You asked me to help you, but you won't fucking work with me. Do you have any idea how much crap you're in, Jase? As it is, we haven't a snowball's chance in hell of getting you out of this. If you won't talk to me, whatever hope we do have becomes even less.'

Jason swore and sat down beside me. 'What do you wanna know?'

'You going off the deep end seems to have happened around the same time Timmy died.'

'So.'

'Could there possibly be a connection?'

'I dunno. Maybe.'

'Maybe?'

I waited for him to gather his thoughts. It had always been like this with him. Answers never came quickly.

'I was upset, of course. I mean, he was my brother, like.'

'Would you be prepared to tell the psychologist that?'

'That fuckin' eejit? All he wants to do is for me to look at spots on paper and fill out stupid forms. He's useless.'

'Yes, but he carries a lot of clout, Jason. What he says could make a difference to how long you have to stay locked up.'

'All right, I'll talk to him.'

'What about your dad?'

'What about him?'

III

'He's left your mum.'

'Ah, he'll be back. He comes and goes.'

'Your mum doesn't seem to think he'll be coming back.'

'You wouldn't want to listen to her. She's a psycho bitch.'

'I've asked her to come on board and work with us. We need you to have a base to go home to, and the only way they'll allow that is if she attends some of the therapy sessions.'

Jason looked at me as if I had lost all reason. 'No fuckin' way. I won't do it, man. She'll screw it all up in some way, and I'll be left in the lurch.'

'You don't have anyone else, Jase,' I said, quietly. 'I wouldn't have gone to her if I could have helped it. There just isn't anyone else I can turn to.'

Jason grabbed my arm tightly. 'What about you? Can't you do it for me?'

'I cannot act as your guardian. I have too many other responsibilities, I can't guarantee to be available to get you to and from meetings – it wouldn't work out. Your mother is unemployed – and let's not forget, she *is* your mother, Jase. That actually does help. It looks good to have family involved in the process. It's like you come from a united, supportive home background.'

Jason shook his head bitterly. 'Shows what they know.' He stood and paced, on edge now. 'I don't like bein' dependent on her, Shane. I'm not one bit happy about it.'

'Give me an alternative. I dunno: grandparents, aunts or uncles, godparents, even. You tell me who, and I'll go and talk to them.'

He continued to stalk up and down in the narrow space, his face a mask of apprehension as he tried to come up with someone else he could turn to. Finally, he had to admit defeat. 'Nobody. Fuck it!'

'Listen to me, Jason,' I said, trying desperately to make him see what was at stake. 'This means the difference between getting to stay here, participate in a programme, and be released in a year, or getting a full custodial sentence, where you will end up out on The Shaker. Believe me, Jase, as tough as you think you are, you will not survive a stretch in that place.'

Jason sat down again, and buried his head in his hands. 'I don't know what to do, Shane.'

I put my arm around him. I felt alone, and tired, and I very much wanted to talk to Ben, to get his advice on whether I was following the right path on this case or not.

'I'm scared, Shane. I'm really afraid of what's going to happen.'

'I know, Jase. I know,' I said.

That made two of us.

18

The Austin was, thankfully, ready when I arrived at the garage and, feeling somewhat more like myself, I turned for home.

The apartment felt too big and empty, so I lit a fire, put on some coffee, and made some dough for bread. I set it aside to prove, then flicked through my CDs to find something soothing to listen to. I came across a disc I hadn't heard in a long time, and put it on. Nic Jones was one of the most celebrated British folk singers and guitarists during the revival of the sixties and seventies. He'd recorded only a few albums when a car crash ended his career. The album *Game Set Match* began with the song 'Bonny Light Horseman', an old ballad that dates back to the Napoleonic era, and deals with a woman whose lover has gone to fight as an infantry-man, but who has not returned from war. There is a verse that, on this particular evening, struck me as especially poignant:

> *If I were some small bird, and had wings and could fly,*
> *I would fly o'er the salt seas where my true love does lie.*
> *And with these fond wings I would beat on his grave*
> *And I'd kiss the fond lips that lie in cold clay.*

Jason was mourning for his brother, who had perpetrated the ultimate betrayal by leaving him through death. He was grieving for a childhood he could never have returned to him. He was trying to overcome a mother and father who had brutalized him, and then confounded their abuse by repeatedly letting him down. There was a part of him that was trying to make sense of all that through raging at the world, visiting abuse on others and repeating patterns of behaviour long-since proven to be unproductive and destructive. I poured myself some more coffee.

In his own, confused way Jason had been trying to locate a place where someone loved him, but had found the task as impossible as if it required changing his form, or growing a pair of wings.

I put the bread in the oven, and then went to the cupboard where I kept my personal notes and files from previous cases. There, behind my autoharp, was a box full of paperwork from my earliest cases. In here were the notes I had made during the court proceedings against Jason Farrell's father. I pulled the dusty box out and brought it into the kitchen. The room was beginning to fill with the smell of baking bread and freshly brewed coffee. I took a bottle of Powers Irish Whiskey from the liquor cabinet, poured a liberal shot into my mug, and began to riffle through the old papers and notebooks.

What caused me to seek out these old musings and hastily scribbled thoughts was that some similarities were starting to emerge for me between that first meeting with Jason and this latest encounter. Both centred on a court case. Each involved a possible betrayal by Timmy. And now, as I sat down to examine a densely lined sheet of paper dated *October 3rd 1991,* I realized that the reliability and good faith of Liz Farrell, Jason's mother, remained a serious question.

I turned my attention to the page.

Jason is going from strength to strength. He really is a remarkable little chap. Despite everything he has been through, he is affectionate, thoughtful and really quite bright. He has no literacy skills, really, but has an amazing memory, and can recall stories almost verbatim. I wish we could send him to school, or even bring in a tutor, but his behaviour can still be erratic at times, and Terri doesn't want to risk it. He doesn't need another setback, at this stage.

The date for the case against his parents has been set – it's to happen at the beginning of next month. I'm dreading it in one way, because it'll be horrible for Jason to have to go through. Terri and I have discussed him being there or not, and we feel it would be better if he didn't attend. But the fallout will be something we can't guard him from. He'll live with the outcome of it for the rest of his life.

His parents are hard people to read. His father is a quite handsome, charming man, in a rough sort of way. It is he who more or less leads the access visits. Liz, the mother, sits back, and says very little. She seems a depressive sort of character. Timmy is like a slightly older version of Jason, except with none of Jason's intrinsic fight or zest for life. If possible, I'd say he is even more damaged that his little brother.

The access visits I organized with Fionn have been erratic to say the least – sometimes his mum and dad show up at the pre-arranged time, other times the mum and brother, Timmy, are there, and sometimes we arrive and there's no sign of any of them. Jason gets dreadfully disappointed when this happens, and I'd ask to stop the visits completely, but for the fact that he just doesn't have any other link to his home and his previous life, and I think that's so important.

Part of me is, in a perverse kind of way, looking forward to the trial, for one reason only: I still know very little about what Jason went through, where he has come from, and even what kind of a real relationship he had with his family. Is there anything worth rebuilding, here? Right now, I don't know.

I put the page aside, and went to the next item in the pile. It was a blue-backed notebook, well thumbed and rumpled, page after page covered front and back in dense lines. The handwriting was scribbled and inaccurate, as if I had written it at great speed, or under extreme pressure. I glanced at the date on the inside cover: *October 21st, 1991.* Not long before the trial. Running my eyes down the first few lines of the page, I remembered why I had been in such a rush to get the details down on paper. I had written these lines on the night when Jason Farrell's life had altered dramatically, and when the entire nature of the approaching court case had changed completely, too.

THEN

19

It was my day off. Darren had come up to the city to visit, and we had a full itinerary of activities planned. My friend had got a job in his chosen field of youth work at a remand and assessment centre in Dublin, and was very happy. He had met a nice girl, looked destined for promotion, and was in every sense a man who knew where he wanted his life to go.

We had been for lunch in a Thai restaurant I had discovered, and were now making our way to a great little second-hand bookshop, which specialized in 1930s and '40s American crime fiction, when I spotted a figure in the crowd whom I thought I recognized. I did a double take, and slowed slightly.

'What is it?' Darren asked.

'See that guy over yonder?'

'The bloke with the little kid?'

'That's him.'

'Yeah.'

'That's the father of my key-child.'

'Really?'

'Yep,' I said. 'And I don't think he has any business with that youngster he's got by the hand.'

Conor Farrell was standing in the entryway of a shopping mall, looking in the window of a toyshop. Holding his hand was a small boy of about three years of age. Farrell was deep in conversation with the child. As I watched, parts of the puzzle clicked into place – there was something very wrong with what I was seeing, and it took only a moment to decipher what that was.

Jason's father was tall and well built, handsome, even, but his clothes were ill-fitting, worn and dirty. His hair was cut so short his scalp could be seen through it, but if he had let it grow, it would have been black, like Jason's and Timmy's. The child he was with was blond, and even from a distance I could see that his clothes were expensive, designer items, and that he was scrupulously clean. I didn't know who this boy was, or where Farrell had found him, but he was certainly not any relative of the man's.

Darren walked back a few paces to stand beside me. 'What do you want to do about this?'

'I'm inclined to confront him.'

'Fair enough. He's not doing anything wrong on the face of it, though.'

'This man abused his son terribly. That kid is not his, I can guarantee you that.'

'It's your call. I'm with you.'

I nodded, and we approached Farrell.

'Conor, hi,' I said, keeping a smile on my face and in my voice.

The man turned. The little boy continued to hold his hand, but his free thumb was stuck in his mouth, and he was sucking it ferociously. I kept eye contact with Farrell, but strained my ears to hear if any hubbub had been raised nearby: a mother calling for a missing child, perhaps. All about were simply the usual sounds of the city, though – if anyone was looking for this tiny, wide-eyed boy, their search had not yet reached this stretch of thoroughfare. Conor was eyeing me with an unreadable expression. He was a volatile man at the best of times, and I knew he was sizing me up to see what I would do, before deciding what his own response might be. We stood like that for a time in silence. I could feel Darren's presence behind me, and was comforted by it. If things descended into violence, one of us could get the boy away while the other subdued Farrell. It would be easier that way.

'So, Conor,' I said, finally, after we had eyeballed one another for a while longer, 'how do I find you this fine afternoon?'

'I'm grand,' he said, not missing a beat. 'It was nice of ye to come over and say hello, but I won't keep you from your business.'

'I'd love to meet your friend first,' I said, motioning towards the little boy with my head.

Conor Farrell glanced momentarily at the child, then smiled at me. I felt like I had just been looked at by a hungry crocodile, and had to suppress a shudder.

'This is Benjy – he's the boy of my neighbour.'

'And does your neighbour know that your own son has been taken into care, Conor?'

The man visibly bristled at that.

'That's nobody's business except my own,' he said through clenched teeth. 'And there is no law that says I can't babysit a friend's boy if he asks me to.'

'He's right,' Darren said quietly behind me.

I nodded, squatted down and looked at the little boy. His eyes were like liquid, his skin pale, almost like porcelain. What kind of neighbour, who took such care of their child, would leave that youngster with a man like Conor Farrell?

I stood and brushed myself down.

'I'm not happy about this, Conor, but there doesn't seem to be a lot I can do about it just now. But know this

– I will be calling your social worker and the police just as soon as I can get to a phone, so I wouldn't be feeling too pleased with yourself.'

Conor said nothing, but led the boy away into the crowd. I remained where I was, shaking my head. I turned to look at Darren, who was watching the two figures, one tall and wiry, the other small and bereft, as they disappeared among the throng.

'This feels all wrong,' I said. 'We should have taken the kid.'

'Why?'

I turned on him, aghast. 'You fucking well know why!'

'Of course I do, you asshole,' he said sharply. 'But it's all down to gut instinct. Yeah, that child, obviously, should not be with that man. But there's always the slim chance that Conor is really babysitting him, with the blessing of both parents. Two complete strangers taking him in the middle of the street would only cause more stress and upset, maybe needlessly.'

I sighed deeply. 'Benjy, if that is his real name, has no business in the company of Conor Farrell. I don't know if he was abducted or what happened, but the situation is just not right.'

'Agreed.'

'Let's go and ring it in,' I said, and we went in search of a payphone.

20

Neither Darren nor I could relax for the rest of the afternoon. We found a quiet bar and had a couple of pints, but our minds remained on the boy Jason's father had called Benjy: who was he, and what strange chain of events had led him to be in the clutches of a known predator? Finally, we gave up on any chance of merry-making, and just went back to the small flat I had rented on the outskirts of the city. There was a phone in the building through which I could be contacted.

By seven that evening there had been no call, though, and I could stand the suspense no longer.

'I'm going in to work, Darren,' I said.

'I'd better stay here,' my friend said, fully aware of the need to safeguard the confidentiality of the other children at The Crow's Nest.

'I'll let you know how things pan out,' I said, and pulled on my coat.

Terri was sitting in her tiny office in the attic of The Crow's Nest, the stub of a hand-rolled cigarette clutched between her teeth, scribbling furiously on a yellow legal pad. I often wondered at how someone as stereotypically beautiful as she was could sometimes look so bizarrely masculine. She glanced up at me when I walked in, a wisp of smoke snaking its way past her nose.

'I hear you're mixed up in this latest mess,' she said. 'Take a seat. We could be here for some time.'

I pulled over the only other chair.

'So, what in the name of the seven snotty orphans happened?' she said, crushing out the cigarette and pulling over her tin to roll another. 'I've had social services, and then the coppers, on to me pretty solidly throughout the afternoon. We just had a visit from a fucking psychologist and the head of the Child Sexual Abuse Assessment team, all looking to see Jase. Which is pretty fucking rich, considering they have wanted sod all to do with him for the last five months.'

'Did you let them talk to him?' I asked, taking the cigarette she offered.

'What do you think, matey?'

'I'd guess not.'

'Give that man a medal,' Terri said drily. 'They'd have scared the kid half to death. We had a pretty heated row, though, out on the lawn, which sent poor Ellen running to lock herself in the shower, seeing as how we were all projecting poisonous brainwaves into her head. And I thought Mark was going to attack them both, he got so wound up. Leo, bless him, just told them not to let the gate hit them on the way out, but I think he was quite upset, really.'

'Not good,' I observed.

'What really grates on me is that these guys are meant to be fucking professionals. What were they thinking?'

'About covering their arses, I reckon.'

'Mmm. You can take that to the bank.'

'Terri,' I said, unable to wait a moment longer. 'What happened to the little boy?'

'The one you spotted Conor with? He's safe back in the bosom of his family, or so I've been told.'

'And they were friends of the Farrells?'

'No. They'd never even heard of him.'

'Then how –'

'First things first,' she interjected. 'How'd you come across our man Conor today?'

There wasn't much to tell, so I got through my story quickly.

'And that's the truth – you just happened across him when you were out with your friend?'

'That's right.'

'You weren't following him, or anything of that nature?'

'What are you getting at, Terri?'

'You're getting pretty close to Jason. You didn't decide to follow Conor until you spotted him up to no good?'

I laughed aloud. 'I was under the impression Conor Farrell had done himself enough damage to seal his fate. No, I did not stalk him or anything of the sort. I was out for a wander with Darren and we happened across him. Now, are you going to let me know how this kid Benjy ended up with him in the first place?'

Terri nodded. 'Okay. It looks like it might just have been a case of wrong place, wrong time. First of all, Benjy isn't the child's name, it's Gearoid. His mother had brought him into the city this afternoon to buy shoes, and they were in the footwear department of Brown Thomas when he went missing.'

'Conor snatched him?'

'Hard to know. He claims he spotted him wandering on the street, and was waiting to see if his parents would turn up.'

'Not what he said to me.'

'I know,' Terri said. 'To be honest, we'd be dubious

about the entire situation, anyway, but his lying to you sort of shows he was up to no good.'

'Did the cops pick him up?'

'Yeah, after you called social services. They informed the police, and there were a couple of uniforms in the area who spotted him and the child in an amusement arcade around an hour later.'

A wave of nausea washed over me. 'An hour?'

Terri sighed deeply. 'Yes.'

'And what were they doing between the time I saw them and they were picked up?'

'We don't know.'

'Has the child been checked out medically?'

'Yes. There's no evidence of any molestation.'

'Has he said anything?'

Terri smiled at me, but it was an expression more of sadness than anything else.

'What?' I asked, the room suddenly seeming impossibly small and close.

'Gearoid hasn't said one word since the police took him in.'

'No fucking way!'

'It could simply be the trauma of being separated from his mother for so long, but . . .'

'. . . but it could be a hell of a lot more than that,' I finished.

'It could. And it begs another question, too.'

'It does?'

'Of course,' Terri said. 'Is this the first time Conor Farrell has "found" a lost child? Or is it the first time he got caught?'

I shook my head and began to roll another cigarette. 'It's a good question,' I said. 'But how do we find out?'

'We use the only access point to the Farrell family we can rely on,' Terri said.

'Jason,' I responded.

'Exactly.'

'He's five years old, Terri. What's he going to be able to tell us?'

Terri stood and made her way to the small window that was set into the roof, which looked out on a sky full of stars. 'If I were you, Shane, I'd use the only language Jason really understands.'

'And what would that be?' I asked.

'Play,' Terri said plainly.

21

The following night, Jason lay tucked up in bed and I sat in a chair by his bedside, a blue notebook in my hand, full of hastily written text.

'You comfy, Jase?'

He nodded.

'Okay. This story is called "The Big House".'

And I began to read a story I had written especially for the occasion:

Once, there was a very big house that someone had built a long time ago on top of a high mountain.

The big house had so many rooms, it was possible to live there all your life and never see all of them. There were rooms full of paintings of beautiful women in gorgeous dresses. Halls could be found crowded with pianos and harpsichords and cellos, all covered in dust, waiting for someone to come and play them. Stairways ran up, up, up, right to the attic, which was cluttered with every kind of junk you could imagine: boxes of books in languages no one ever spoke any more, old chairs with no legs and the stuffing coming out, an ancient gramophone that didn't have a motor, and far too many other things to mention. The stairs also went down, down, down, right to the cellar, damp and cold and darker than the blackest night.

In the big house lived Mary and her dad. Mary was nine. She had been born in the house and had never been anywhere else. Mary's mother had died when she was still a baby. Her dad was a scientist, and he was very clever. Mary spent most mornings doing lessons – reading, sums, history, geography and science (her father was also her teacher, because the nearest school was very far away, on the other side of the mountain) – but during the afternoon she would explore the house and play with her dolls, and her dad would go to his laboratory and do experiments. Mary sometimes asked him what the experiments were about, but he always laughed and told her it was much too complicated for her to ever understand. She didn't think that was much of an answer, but it was what he always said, so after a while, Mary stopped asking.

Mary loved her father, but she would have been very lonely in the big house if it weren't for her best friend, Spindle. Spindle was a mouse and, just like her, he had been born in the big house and had lived his whole life there. Spindle went everywhere with Mary, and at night, he slept in a matchbox on her bedside table. Mary told Spindle everything, all her hopes and dreams, and Spindle never laughed or made fun of her.

So Mary, her father and little Spindle were very happy.

'That must be some big house,' Jason said.
    'Yeah – it was really, really big,' I agreed.
    'Bigger than The Crow's Nest?'
    'Much bigger than that.'
    'Was it big as a king's palace?'
    I thought about that. 'Bigger than that even, I'd say.'
    'That's big,' Jason said.

One night there was a terrible storm. The rain lashed down and made a sound against the windows like thousands of little fists all banging, trying to get in. Dark-grey clouds covered the sky, and thunder, so loud it made Mary's ears hurt, crashed and banged all over the mountain. Lightning ripped the rain clouds open, lighting up the night so that Mary and Spindle, who were huddled up together under a blanket, gazing out the window of her bedroom, could see the tiny, narrow road that wound its way up from the little village under the mountain. Suddenly, Spindle whispered: 'Mary, who's that coming up the mountain?'

Mary peered down, and sure enough, when the next flash of lightning lit up the world, Mary could see a figure far down below, all bundled up in a heavy coat, with what looked like a bag over his shoulder.

'Who would come out on a night like this?' Mary asked.

The wind was blowing so hard the person had to lean right into it to stop being blown off the mountainside to their death.

'Where do you think he is going?' Spindle asked her in his quiet way.

Mary thought about this, because it was a good question.

'There is only one place for him to go,' she said at last. 'He must be coming to our big house.'

They watched for a long time as the person on the road gradually came closer and closer, getting bigger and bigger as each flash of lightning made the rocky place as bright as day. At last, Spindle and Mary heard: BANG! BANG! BANG! Someone was knocking on the huge wooden door of the big house.

'He is here,' Mary said and, picking up her little friend and putting him on her shoulder, the girl ran out on to the landing, so she could see who it was.

BANG! BANG! BANG! came the knocks again. Mary and Spindle heard footsteps, and the sound of complaining, and Mary's dad came down the hallway from his laboratory.

'Who is knocking on such a night?' he called, wiping something from his hands as he clattered over the stone floor and placed his hand on the great doorknob.

'Let me in, for the love of God!' came a voice from outside. (Mary and Spindle could barely hear it, because the wind was screeching underneath the door and the windows all around the big house were rattling and banging.)

Mary's dad flung open the door, and the strange man almost fell inside. They both had to struggle against the wind to get the door closed, but together they did, and then the stranger fell to the floor, exhausted, a puddle of freezing water spreading about him from his soaked clothes.

'Welcome, stranger,' Mary's dad said, looking down at the man.

'Do you not know me, Arthur?' the strange man asked, his voice raspy with exhaustion after his long climb through the storm.

Mary's dad seemed very surprised, and took a step back.

'Marcus?' he asked.

The visitor pulled his hood back, and from where she sat, Mary could see that he looked very like her father.

'Hello, brother,' Marcus said. 'I have come to stay.'

'Is him gonna be nice?' Jason asked.

'You'll have to wait and see,' I said. 'It's a story, so anything can happen.'

'That mouse talks,' Jason said, his eyes wide. 'Is he magic?'

'He is if you want him to be,' I said.

'Okay. Go on.'

The next morning, Mary's dad introduced her to their guest.

'This is your uncle Marcus, my little brother.'

'Hello, Mary,' Uncle Marcus said, shaking her hand (Mary liked this – it made her feel grown-up). 'I am very pleased to meet you.'

'Uncle Marcus will be staying with us for a while,' Mary's dad said. 'Won't that be nice?'

Marcus was a little bit taller than Mary's father, and he had long hair with no grey in it, and a face with fewer lines. When he laughed, his whole body shook as if the laughter had filled him up and was trying to burst out, and that made Mary laugh too.

Marcus knew all kinds of games, and he never got bored playing them. Mary's dad would have breakfast with them each morning, then off he would go to his laboratory. It seemed that, now that Marcus was there, he didn't feel the need to give Mary her lessons.

'Well, Mary, what'll we do today?' Marcus would ask. Mary would already have something in mind, and they would always play her game first – Hide and Seek, or Pin-the-Tail-on-the-Donkey, or Skittles – but after that, there would be one of Marcus's games, and they were always wonderful. In the bag he had carried up the mountain he had the most marvellous toys. There were balls that came back to you when you bounced them, and little wind-up men that danced and sang and liked to be chased (they made lovely squeaking noises as they shot about the floor). He had a Draughts game with pieces that moved by themselves when you pointed to the square you wanted them to go to, and made a kind of *boing* sound when they jumped to take another piece. Every day there was a different game and a new, exciting toy. Mary often wondered how Marcus fitted all these things in his bag. But she was having such fun she decided not to ask him. Marcus was her father's brother, after all, and Dad usually didn't like being asked questions.

'Him *is* nice,' Jason said.

'He seems that way,' I said.

134

One night, when Marcus had been living with them at the big house for three months, Spindle woke Mary up. He did this by nibbling her ear with his little sharp teeth.

'Ouch,' Mary said. 'What's wrong? Did you have a bad dream again?'

'No,' whispered Spindle. 'I want to talk to you.'

'What about?'

'Uncle Marcus.'

Mary sat up and put Spindle on her knee so that they could see one another properly. 'Go on, then.'

'I don't like him, Mary. He smells funny, and there's something strange about the way he looks at you. He scares me.'

Mary laughed. 'No, Spindle, he's lovely. He has the best toys I've ever seen, and he always listens to what I've got to say, and anyway, he's Dad's brother. If there was anything nasty about him, surely Dad would know.'

'I don't trust him,' Spindle said. 'I wish he'd just go away, and that things would go back to the way they were.'

'Well I hope he stays forever,' Mary said, putting Spindle back on to the bedside table and snuggling under her blankets again. 'And I think you might be a little bit jealous.'

Spindle said nothing, but he decided there and then that he would keep a very close eye on Marcus.

'That mouse don't like the Marcus guy,' Jason said, his eyes now heavy with sleep.

'No, he doesn't.'

'I hope Mary will be all right.'

'You need to go to sleep, now,' I said. 'We'll read some more tomorrow night.'

Jason nodded, closed his eyes, and was asleep in moments.

22

When I went downstairs I found Clara, a worker from one of the other teams, sitting at the kitchen table sipping tea. I had agreed to come in outside my usual hours to work with Jason during the run-up to the trial, primarily to see if I could glean any details from him about his life at home, or shed any light on Conor's abduction of Gearoid.

Clara was in her late fifties and matronly in that warm, plump, powerfully gentle way some women have. This was offset by an incisive intelligence that made her someone the entire team often went to for advice and guidance, and a person we all listened to whenever she offered an opinion.

'Jason settled?' she asked.

'Sleeping like a baby,' I said.

'What's this story business all about?' Clara said. 'Terri told me it was vitally important that you put him to bed tonight, and that no one but you was to read to him. Now, I don't want to overstate matters, but I read a pretty good story.'

'We're trying to get him to start talking about his life at home,' I said. 'I've written something that I hope will get him thinking about what he's been through.'

'Bit of an author, are we?'

I laughed. 'No. I did a few classes on therapeutic stories while I was at college. I suppose we're seeing if I can put some of it into action. I just hope it works.'

'You go on home, then,' Clara said. 'You're on with Sarah tomorrow at ten. A young fella like you should be living a little, not spending every spare moment in here.'

I smiled and patted the back of her hand where it lay on the table top.

'I'll head off in a minute or two,' I said. 'Where's Una?' I was referring to Clara's co-worker.

'She's taken Mark and Ellen to the cinema. Leo's gone to bed early, so it's just me and the Red Lady for the rest of the evening.'

'Don't tell me you've fallen for that old story,' I laughed, pouring myself some tea from the pot she had sitting on a coaster in front of her.

'It's not a story,' Clara said matter-of-factly. 'I've seen her several times.'

'Come on,' I said. 'You don't expect me to believe you and Una –'

'I never said anything about Una,' Clara said. 'Una hasn't seen her yet.'

'Just you, then?'

'No. Terri's seen her. So has Bernice.' Bernice was a worker who did some overnight shifts for us from time to time.

'I'm kind of jealous, now,' I said in mock offence. 'Why do you think she's so selective?'

Clara brought her cup over to the sink. 'Well, I've thought about that, and I believe you have to be in a certain frame of mind. The mood has to be right.'

'How do you mean?'

Clara sat back down and pondered my question. 'Well, when Bernice saw her, she'd just had a really tough night with Ellen – the poor thing had been in a frenzy of paranoia, and Bernice had been sitting up for hours with her.

She finally got the child to sleep, and came downstairs and nodded off sitting on the couch. She woke up in the dark, around five in the morning, and there was the Red Lady, standing by the fireplace. Bernice said they looked at one another for a good minute, and then she just ... wasn't there any more.'

'And Terri?'

'Ah, Terri is a little reticent about sharing her experience,' Clara said. 'When I mentioned that I'd seen her, Terri wasn't one bit surprised, and just said, "Yeah, me too," as if it was the most normal thing in the world. Wouldn't say more than that, though.'

I was fascinated. 'So, what about you, then?'

'Well, I'd just been woken by Leo, who'd had one of his accidents. You know the way he's usually fairly devil-may-care about it, but this evening he was tired and, well, it was just like he'd had enough of it all. When I got him back into bed, he got a bit teary, so I sat and we talked quietly for an hour or so. He spoke to me about how he sometimes dreamed about what his parents are like, and how, when he tries really hard, he thinks he can almost remember his mother's voice.'

'He said that?'

'Yeah, he did.'

'He's a complex one, our Leo.'

'That's for sure. So, when he finally dozed off, I went to go back to bed, but just as I got to the end of the hallway, I thought I caught a glimpse of something moving through the door of the living room. Of course, I thought it was another of the children up, so I went in there, ready to deal with Mark all a-fluster, or Ellen sleepwalking. When I went into that room, the moon was shining in and the place was lit up like it was day. She was standing with her back to me, looking out at the garden. You know, I froze there, not sure what to do, and sort of blinking, dead sure my eyes were playing tricks on me. Slowly, like she was floating, rather than moving, she turned to me.'

'What did she look like?' I asked, my voice hushed.

'She was young. She'd long blonde hair, sort of clipped up at the sides, and she was wearing what looked like an expensive party dress – old-fashioned, from the turn of the century, perhaps – in a deep, dark red. She looked terribly sad. Sad and lovely.'

'Were you scared?'

'No, funnily, enough. Bernice said the same thing. There was nothing frightening about her. She reminded me of one of the children, in a way. I wanted to go over and hold her. She looked like she could use a hug.'

A light rain brushed against the window. 'So what happened?'

'One moment she was there, large as life. The next, she just wasn't. I don't remember seeing her disappear. It's hard to describe.'

'You're not spinning me a yarn now, are you, Clara?' I asked.

'I paid a visit to the library after I saw her,' the older woman said. 'This house has seen a lot of suffering. Being here with the children and all the intense emotions they bring with them – well, I think they might have stirred something.'

'And you've seen her more than once?'

'Three times, in all.'

'Well, I think it's an experience I can do without,' I said, standing. 'I'm going home to sleep for a few hours before I'm due in here again.'

'Good idea.'

I peeped in at the empty sitting room on my way out. If the Red Lady was in there, she was hiding.

23

Jason and I sat out in the garden, under the big ash tree
that grew behind The Crow's Nest.

'I'd like to explore today,' Uncle Marcus said the next morning
after breakfast. 'There are so many rooms in this big house, we
should see what strange and interesting things we can find.'

Mary had not played Explorers for a while, so she said:
'Okay. Let's make some sandwiches and take them with us. We
can have a picnic.'

So Mary made them some cheese sandwiches and took
some apples from the bowl on the kitchen table. Then off they
went.

For the first hour or so, the rooms they passed through were
all ones Mary had seen. Marcus spent a long time in a room
full of maps of countries with strange names all over the walls,
and she was a little bit bored. In another room there were racks
with hundreds of dusty bottles stacked right up to the ceiling.
Marcus blew the dust off one and held it up to the light. 'Do
you know what this is, Mary?' he asked her.

'No,' Mary said. 'Is it lemonade?'

'It's much better than that,' Marcus smiled. 'We'll take one
of these for our picnic. You'll love it.'

By the time they stopped to eat their sandwiches, Mary was
very bored, and tired of walking and climbing stairs, so she
was glad to sit down. They found a room with a big table and
comfy chairs and a thick rug on the floor made of some kind
of animal's fur, and they spread out the food between them.

Marcus took a penknife from his pocket, and used it to pull the cork out of the bottle. He took a long drink from it. 'That's the stuff,' he said. 'Try some.'

Mary took the bottle from him, and took a sip. She had never tasted anything quite like it. It was kind of sweet and sour and bitter and burny all at the same time. She spat it out right away.

'Oh, it's horrible!' she said, taking a big bite of her apple to get rid of the taste.

Marcus laughed and had another drink. 'It's wine, Mary. Grown-ups drink it. I thought you were mature enough to like it. I must have been wrong.'

Mary blushed at that, and felt angry and embarrassed. She liked Marcus and wanted to be his friend. He could act like a child sometimes, and play with her as if he were nine years old, like she was; but he treated her like an adult too, now and then, and spoke to her as if he cared what she thought. She wanted him to believe she was clever and sensible.

'She shouldn't drink that stuff,' Jason said.

'But her uncle wants her to,' I said. 'He's a grown-up. Shouldn't she do what a grown-up asks her?'

'Not . . . not always . . .' Jason said.

'Why not?'

Jason said nothing for a while. He was lying with his head resting against my leg. It was not a warm afternoon, but we were wrapped up with hats and scarves, and I wanted to be close to the house, in case the story stimulated anything in the boy. Finally, Jason said: 'Sometimes, grown-ups can be bad.'

'Can they?' I asked.

'Yeah.' He paused. 'Keep reading.'

'I was only joking,' Mary laughed. 'Here, pass the bottle back over.'

And she put it to her lips and took a great big gulp. It was so nasty she thought for a moment that she would be sick, but she swallowed as quickly as she could, and smiled at Uncle Marcus.

'That's my girl,' he said.

It wasn't long before Mary began to feel strange: a little bit dizzy and sort of sleepy too. She found it hard to listen to what Marcus was saying, and she kept giggling, even though there was nothing to laugh at. After a few drinks, the wine didn't seem to taste as bad, and she drank as much as she could, to show Marcus that she really was grown-up. They finished the sandwiches, and then Marcus said: 'Let's have a little rest, shall we? Help me push this table back, and we can lie on the floor. The rug is nice and thick, it'll be like a mattress.'

They stretched out, side by side. Mary saw that, in this room, someone long ago had painted a picture of a little girl on the ceiling. She was sitting on a swing that hung from a big tree in a field of red flowers, and she looked very sad and lonely. Mary wanted to give her a hug, and tell her that there was no need to be sad. She was here now, and so was Marcus, and Spindle was nearby somewhere (he hadn't been around her so much, since they'd had their talk, but she had spotted him now and then throughout the day, watching her from a window sill or a skirting board). There were plenty of good friends here in the big house to play with.

'Doesn't that girl look sad?' Mary said, and her voice sounded funny.

'Would you like to play a game?' Marcus said, as if he had not heard her. 'A game for grown-ups?'

Mary really didn't feel much like playing just then. She was very sleepy. But she did want to make Marcus happy.

'Is it a good game?' she asked, and now it was hard to speak – the words seemed difficult to say.

'Oh, it's the best game of them all,' Marcus said. He was leaning over her, his face very close. 'Your dad wouldn't want me to show you this game. He'd say you're too young. But we know better, don't we? It can be our secret.'

'Yes. I like secrets,' Mary said.

So Marcus showed her.

Jason had sat up and was looking at me intently.

'What he do?' he asked.

'I think he hurt her,' I said. 'He did things adults shouldn't do to children. Things that are bad for children.'

Jason considered this seriously. He didn't seem upset by the story – it was as if he understood perfectly what was happening. 'Kissin' and stuff like that,' he said. 'Touchin' in secret places.'

'Yes,' I said. 'Just like that.'

'Yeah,' he nodded. 'That's bad for children, so it is. Bad things to do.'

That night, Spindle sat on Mary's bedside table.

'Mary, you must tell your father,' he said quietly. 'There are some games children should never play.'

Mary was wrapped up in her blanket, and could not look at the mouse. She hurt inside and felt sick and frightened. 'But Marcus is my friend,' she said.

'He hurt you, Mary,' Spindle whispered. 'He made you drink wine and then did things adults do. Private things; games that are not fun for children.'

Mary sobbed then. 'No. The game was not fun at all.'

'You must tell your father.'

'Okay. But I do not want Dad to be angry with him. He was

just trying to show me how grown-ups play. I do not want him to go away. I have liked all the other games we played.'

'Your father must decide if he stays in the big house or not,' Spindle said. 'But Marcus is his little brother. I am sure they will work things out.'

Mary and Spindle went to the scientist's room early the next morning before breakfast, but he was not there. They found him in his laboratory, stirring something purple in a steel pot over a flame.

'Mary, I have told you not to come down here,' he said when she came in. 'And please stop bringing that dirty little mouse all about the place with you. It is very unhygienic.'

Mary went over to her father and put her hand on his arm.

'Dad, I need to talk to you about something.'

'Yes, yes. I'll be up for breakfast in a little bit. Uncle Marcus will chat with you until then.'

'But it's Uncle Marcus I want to talk to you about,' Mary said, and her eyes filled up with tears. Somehow, what Marcus had done made her feel different, like she was not really a little girl any more. She was also frightened that her dad would be angry with her about what had happened, even though she had not done anything wrong.

'What's wrong, child?' Mary's dad said, when he saw she was upset. He was a bit gruff sometimes, but he did love his daughter. 'Why, come here and sit down. What's all this fuss about?'

Mary sat on one of the wooden stools her father kept in the laboratory, and then she told him about Marcus and the game they had played. Mary's father stayed very quiet while she spoke, and as he listened his face became paler and paler and he made his hands into fists and squeezed them very tight. When she had finished telling, he cleared his throat loudly, and turned away from her, so she was looking at his back.

'Now, Mary,' he said, and his voice sounded like he had a bad cold all of a sudden, 'I'm sure you must have made a mistake. Marcus is very fond of you. He would never do something like that.'

'He did, though, Daddy,' Mary said, and even though she tried very hard not to cry, she began again. 'I'm telling you the truth.'

'I don't think you're lying,' said her dad, and he turned back to face her, and he looked old and scared. 'I just think . . . well, you told me you'd been drinking from one of the bottles in the Wine Room. Now, you know you shouldn't do that, but I'm not cross about it. I should have told you. I expect you just had a bad dream.'

Mary was confused now. Maybe she had dreamed it all. Marcus had always been nice to her.

'I don't know,' she said. 'I was sure it was real.'

Her dad came over and gave her a hug, which was something he rarely did. He smelled of chemicals and aftershave. It felt nice, not like when Marcus had touched her in the bad game. 'It's all right, my love. We all get mixed up from time to time. You're only nine and wine is not meant to be drunk by children. Why don't I lock up the laboratory for today and we can go for a walk in the mountains, like we used to when you were little?'

'I'd like that,' Mary said.

So he took off his white coat and hung it on a hook on the door, and they went upstairs to breakfast. Marcus was already there at the table, and he looked surprised to see them come up from the laboratory together. Mary's dad was very quiet and barely looked at him, and so Mary, who usually sat next to her uncle, made sure to sit across the table from him, near her dad, but Marcus joked and talked just like always, and didn't seem to notice.

Jason was angry this time. 'Why him not b'lieve her?'

'Sometimes adults don't understand,' I explained. 'Or they don't want to know. And that can be hard. But you know what? That doesn't matter. If something bad happens to you, you tell, and you keep telling until an adult *does* believe you. And sooner or later, somebody will.'

'But he's her daddy! He has to!'

I took a deep breath, and bit the bullet. 'Sometimes, mammies and daddies aren't the right people to tell, though, are they?' I asked. 'They don't always look after their kids as well as they should.'

Jason leaped to his feet, his face crumpled in fury.

'What're you sayin'?'

'I'm saying that mammies and daddies are often the ones that hurt their children the most,' I said. 'It doesn't mean they don't love them, it just means they made a mistake. And they can be terrible mistakes, which hurt the children very badly.'

Jason kicked me as hard as he could. It didn't hurt much. The anger in his teary eyes did, though. 'That's a mean story you're tellin' me,' he said. 'I don't wanna hear no more of it, see?'

And he turned tail and ran into the house. I sat where I was for a while longer, wondering if *I* had just made a big mistake.

NOW

24

Kris Isaacson was blond, with thinning hair and a paunch that even his well-cut suit could not contain. He seemed bored as he spread papers out on the table in St Phelim's cold, echoing conference room. Jason was jumpy and nervy. I wondered if he had been doing more drugs during recent months than he had been letting on: he gave the impression of someone suffering withdrawal.

It was ten thirty in the morning, but the sky was so overcast the room was gloomy, dark and inhospitable. Kris Isaacson sighed in apparent apathy and sat heavily down at the top of the table.

'There is not much I can do here,' he said, his accent a peculiar mixture of inner-city Dublin and something else – Scandinavian perhaps. 'You are going to plead guilty to these crimes, yes?'

Isaacson was the lawyer for the health service. It seemed that this case was low on his list of priorities.

'I'm not pleadin' guilty to *nuthin'*!' Jason growled.

'For Christ's sake, we discussed this!' I snapped. 'There is nothing to be gained from denying the charge. Anyway, you *did* do it. You told me as much yourself.'

'I'm not sayin' anythin' until I see me solicitor,' Jason (who had obviously been watching far too much television) said, crossing his arms tightly and lowering his head.

'This is your fucking lawyer, Jason!' I said in exasperation.

'There's really not a whole lot I can do here,' the corpulent legal eagle said again. 'This case is really just a formality.'

'Why don't you just go, then?' I snapped.

'Yes, I think I will,' Isaacson said, gathering his paperwork as quickly as he could.

'You won't fuckin' catch me pleadin' guilty,' Jason muttered.

When Isaacson had gone, I looked at the young man, who still sat sulking across the table from me.

'What the hell was all that about?' I asked. 'Are you completely insane? There are very, very few people on your side, here, and that guy is being paid to speak up on your behalf. Why in the name of everything sacred would you go out of your way to alienate him?'

Jason said nothing for a moment, then turned to me with a contemptuous look. '*That* guy couldn't give a shite about me,' he said. 'I might as well get up there and defend meself as throw me lot in with the likes of him.'

'Believe me, Jason, that would not be a very good idea,' I said wearily.

'I'd do a better job than that fat cunt.'

There wasn't much to say to that. Jason was probably right.

I stood and walked over to the glass partition that separated us from the corridor outside. It was empty, and as sparsely decorated as the room we were in. 'Why'd you attack the old woman, Jason?' I asked. My voice held no accusation, no anger – just tired resignation. 'You were an angry kid when we were in The Crow's Nest, but you were *decent*. You *cared* about people. The Jason I knew then, he wouldn't have done something like that. These past few days, all I'm wondering about is how you came to be the kind of person who would beat up and sexually assault an old lady who never so much as looked crooked at you.' I turned back to look at him, and when he averted his gaze, I moved until I was in his line of vision again. 'Explain it to me, Jase. If you want me to keep coming here, to continue to represent you like I've been doing, I think you owe it to me.'

'I don't know!' he shouted, tears starting to run down his pocked cheeks.

I lunged over and grabbed him by the front of his hoody. 'That's bullshit, Jason,' I said through clenched teeth. 'Nobody does anything without thinking it through, even if only for a moment. There would have been some point when you were in her home when you realized that you could go through with raping her, or you could walk away from it.'

'No!'

I shook him, a fury building up in me now. I wasn't hurting the boy, but I was angry. He needed to be honest with himself much more than he needed to be honest with me. The time had come to face what he'd done once and for all. With or without Isaacson, he'd be no good in front of a judge if he was unable to feel remorse for the crimes he had committed.

'Yes! Yes, Jason, you think long and hard about it.'

'Let me go, you bastard!'

'Not until you start talking to me. We sort this out right now, or I'm out that door and I'm not coming back.'

'All right, all right!'

'What?' I shook him again, feeling like a complete heel, but knowing I had to force his hand, or everything was lost. 'All right to what, Jason?'

'You're right. I didn't have to hit her, or fuck her up like I did.'

'So why did you, then?'

He looked at me, snot running from his nose into the patchy stubble on his upper lip, his lower lip trembling fiercely. This was it: he knew that, for us to move forward, he would have to articulate what he had done; he would have to admit what he had become.

'I did it because I wanted to,' he whispered.

I let go his top and stepped back, suddenly unsure where to go. 'You wanted to do what?'

'I wanted to do to her what was done to me.'

My voice sounded far away when I spoke. I felt as if I was looking down on myself from above. 'But she didn't do anything to you. Neither did the children you hurt.'

'Every time I done that, it was like a little bit of the pain in me was put in them, and I'd feel better for a while.'

I sat down on the table. The room was full of hurting and anger. You could almost smell it. 'For a while?'

'It was like there was a hole inside me that was full up of sickness, and every time I'd empty a little bit out, it would just fill right back up again,' Jason said. 'It doesn't matter what I try to do, I can't never get rid of it all.'

I nodded and found that I couldn't look at him. I went over to the door. 'You can go on back to your room,' I said. 'I'll call in later.'

'Shane –'

'Yeah,' I said, with my back still towards him.

'Can you help me make it go away?'

'I don't know, Jason,' I said, and I went out, closing the door behind me.

25

Andrew Roche, the psychologist who would be co-ordinating Jason's treatment programme, met me for lunch later that same day. He was tall, handsome and tanned, dressed in an open-necked shirt and designer jeans. He was already at a table, eating some poached salmon when I came in. He stood, shook my hand, and waited for me to slip into the chair opposite before he sat down again.

'So, how is Jason progressing?' he asked, when I'd ordered a bowl of soup and some breads.

'Hard to articulate,' I admitted. 'I'm inclined to say that we made some headway this morning, but I'm not so sure I didn't mess things up royally.'

I told him about what had happened.

'You didn't do anything wrong,' Andrew said. 'You were honest. From what I've been told, you've been straight with him from the beginning. He's lucky to have you at all – you don't need to be taking the role you've adopted.'

I shook my head. 'Yes, I do.'

'Why?'

'I don't believe in leaving a job undone.'

He sat back, a bemused expression on his face. 'So what, your involvement is rooted in a sense that you've started, so you'd better finish?'

I shrugged. 'I suppose you could put it like that.'

Andrew Roche laughed a good, hearty laugh. 'That,

Shane, is an absolutely ridiculous reason to be working with this young man. You do know that, don't you?'

My food arrived and I tried some. It was good, but I still felt drained from the morning, and hadn't much appetite. 'Look, I used to be close to this boy. It was a long time ago, and a lot of things have happened since then, but in *his* head nothing has changed,' I said. 'We all do what we do for different reasons. So, maybe I've got an odd system of values. And I don't deny that I probably do. But then, you've probably got your own foibles and quirks.'

Andrew nodded and continued with his lunch. 'You're right, of course. Sometimes I can't help being fascinated by what makes people tick.'

'You're excused,' I said.

'So how can I help you today?' he asked.

'I really want to know how absolutely vital it is for Jason's mother to be involved in his therapy sessions.'

Andrew continued to work at his meal, but I sensed him tensing ever so slightly.

'Well, Shane, I thought everyone was absolutely clear that, without a designated external support figure, the course of therapy we're proposing just won't work.'

'Okay, but couldn't we try to find another way around that?'

The psychologist motioned for more coffee, and fixed his gaze on me. 'For example?'

'What if the services of the Dunleavy Trust were at Jason's disposal?'

'I don't follow.'

'I could attend the sessions with him, but I'm not going to pretend that I'd be available around the clock when he gets out of Phelim's. But if I could get one or two of the other workers to agree to be on-call when I'm indisposed, well, then, there'd always be somebody for him to turn to, wouldn't there?'

Andrew poured some milk into his freshly replenished cup. 'And Jason has as close a relationship with these other workers as he does with you?'

'Not yet, but –'

'And they would be prepared to adopt a residential style of work with him for the foreseeable future? He needs a completely stable and supportive environment.'

'No, but –'

'And they would all attend the group work with him, each and every session?'

'Um . . . no . . .'

Andrew spread his hands and smiled.

'I think you have just answered your own question, Shane.'

'Yes, but –'

'The entire purpose of the therapeutic intervention we apply is to help both the offender and their family to get used to the nature of the abusive mentality. Sexual offenders are manipulative, opportunistic and quite narcissistic. Jason will try to twist and bend the will of whoever he lives with to suit his own ends. His support person needs to be prepared to be firm and resolute in reflecting all these behaviours back at him and, more importantly, to be equipped to identify such patterns of activity as they occur. I very much prefer family members or primary carers to take on the support role, as they are best placed to spot personality traits and head them off at the pass, so to speak. As you have some past experience with Jason, I'd take you at a stretch, but frankly, your colleagues probably don't know this boy from Adam, and therefore would not be suitable. Are you prepared to foster Jason, Shane? Have him move in with you?'

'No.'

'Well, I think the conversation has reached its end, then, don't you?'

He was right, and we both knew it.

26

The Benjamin family lived in a large, homely house in a pleasant suburb of the city. They had fostered Jason in 1999 and, despite that experience, had continued to take children in need into their home. Clarissa Benjamin was in her mid-forties, and met me at the door with a smile. She was probably not five feet in height, and couldn't weigh much more than a child herself, but I got a sense of inner strength, courage and warmth from her. She offered me coffee, and when we were seated in her untidy-but-cosy kitchen, began to speak about Jason Farrell.

'I've known children from all sorts of backgrounds and of all ages, Mr Dunphy,' she said. 'When kids come into our home they are all treated the exact same: we have no favourites and we don't stand on ceremony. He was just thirteen years old when he arrived here, and there was trouble right from day one. We knew he'd come from a special unit for children with behavioural problems, but we'd been told he had sorted out his issues, and we'd spent a lot of time with him before he made the move. Me and Frank, my husband, wouldn't have offered to take him if we didn't think it would work. But we were wrong. Badly wrong.'

'How?'

'Nicola has been with us since she was a baby. She was six when Jason came to stay. He developed an unhealthy attitude to her right from the off. He'd steal her underwear, expose himself to her, try to sneak into her room at night – it got so that we had to take her into our room to sleep. He was furious about that.'

'Did you talk to him about it?' I asked.

'Of course we did. We tried every approach we could think of. We were understanding, we got cross, we did the whole disappointed thing – nothing worked. He seemed to respond better to me than he did to Frank. To be honest with you, he scarcely acknowledged that Frank existed.'

'But I'm sure you'd encountered tough kids before,' I said.

'Oh, we weren't really that upset by his failure to settle in,' Clarissa said. 'I thought it would just be a matter of time, and then he'd see that we weren't going to give up on him, and he'd come around.'

'And he never showed any sign of responding to you even a little bit?'

'I remember going into his room to check on him one night. When I stuck my head in the door, I thought he was asleep. I went over, pulled the quilt up over him – tucked him in, you know – and I was just going back out when he said, in a voice that was wide awake: "You're not my mother."'

'What did you do?'

'I told him I knew that, that I just wanted to be his friend, that he was safe with us, and would be for as long as he wanted our house to be his home.'

'What'd he say?'

'He said that he would never, ever call it home. He said it didn't matter what we did, or what we said, or what we gave him or did for him, he hated us.'

'Ouch,' I said. 'That couldn't have been pleasant to hear.'

Clarissa laughed and poured herself some more coffee. 'I'm not going to tell you it was easy. I cried myself to sleep that night.'

'I'm sorry.'

She waved away my condolence. 'We started getting complaints from the school. He'd kept his head down, but I sort of knew he was beginning to spiral out of control. Or maybe he wasn't – maybe, somewhere in his subconscious, it was all part of some grand scheme. I don't know. I don't pretend to understand what makes Jason Farrell tick.'

'What sort of complaints were they?'

'It started off much like the other children we've had – fighting, bullying, name-calling. But then the letters home started to outline much more disturbing things: smearing faeces in the toilets, making himself vomit in class, forcing another child to eat dog excrement. Then the teacher found him locked into a toilet cubicle with a child from one of the junior classes – a little boy with a learning disability. He had him naked to the waist, and I dread to think what might have happened if he had not been discovered.'

'What did you do?'

'I took him out of school immediately. He never went back.'

The window of the kitchen looked out on a back garden full of play equipment: swings, slides, tricycles, a sandpit, a large trampoline with a protective mesh all around it. It looked like such a cheerful place, it was hard to believe that the experiences this tiny woman was describing had happened there. The Benjamin family, I thought, should be immune from such horrors.

'The Whittys lived next door, and they were our

friends,' Clarissa continued. 'I could show you photo albums of holidays we went on together. Joshua Whitty is Nicola's godfather. You know, he hasn't seen her since it happened.'

A single tear trickled down her cheek, though her voice remained steady and her breathing even. I knew I had made a mistake coming to see her. Clarissa did not need to be reminded of what Jason Farrell had done to her family and those they loved.

'Jason had been sitting right where you are now, colouring in a book Frank had brought home. I remember he had bought him a lovely wooden box full of pencils of every shade you could imagine, the kind that, if you dipped them in water, they'd paint, too.'

'Yeah, I know the ones you mean,' I said, somehow feeling I had to affirm what she was saying to account for my being there.

'We didn't want him to feel bad about being taken out of school. Somehow, we still thought we could turn him around. I went out to take some clothes in from the line, and when I came back inside, he was gone. I thought he'd gone to the loo, or to watch television, so it was maybe six or seven minutes later before I started to wonder where he was. It was a good half-hour before we found him. By then it was too late.'

She cleared her throat and stood up to clear away the coffee things. 'Little Gertie was only two. Jason went in through the back door – he knew they left it open during the day. It seems he found Gertie in the playroom, and took her upstairs. Even when she cried out, he didn't stop. Ethel, who had been in the sitting room, talking to a friend on the phone, heard her crying, and went to see what was wrong. He . . . continued to penetrate the child even when her mother came into the room. She had to drag him off.'

'He was placed in a programme, after that?'

'They took him away that night. I wasn't sorry.'

'And the Whittys?'

'They always said they didn't hold us responsible, but they sold their home for way below the asking price and moved away within the month. Gertie ... she needed stitches.'

We remained silent while she rinsed the cups and placed them in the dishwasher.

'I hope you found whatever answers you're looking for,' she said, when she had finished.

'I don't even know what the questions are,' I said.

'You tell me he's in trouble again.'

'Yes.'

'What kind of trouble?'

'The kind that could see him locked away for a long time.'

Clarissa sighed. 'I'm not sorry,' she said. 'I know that's not what you want to hear, but it's the truth.'

'Do you know, I came here to ask you to help him, to perhaps foster him again,' I said.

'Did you?'

'I did.'

'You must be pretty desperate.'

I smiled. 'You have no idea.'

'He's too damaged to fix, Mr Dunphy,' Clarissa said. 'It might be kinder to him if you faced up to that.'

THEN

27

Curiosity got the better of Jason.

'I wants to hear what happened to Mary,' he said gruffly.

'Are you sure?'

'Yeah. You tell me the rest.'

We sat side by side on beanbags in the playroom.

'Remember Mary had just tried to tell her dad what Uncle Marcus had done?' I reminded Jason.

'Yeah. I remember. He din' b'lieve her.'

Mary's dad took the rest of that day off, and didn't go to his laboratory the following day either. Marcus kept away from them, disappearing into the endless rooms of the big house. Mary thought that perhaps he would go and live in another part of the house, and that she might not ever see him again. While that thought made her a little bit sad, it was also sort of comforting, and she began to relax a bit. It was almost like what had happened was a dream.

'I must go back to work today,' her father told her one morning at breakfast. 'Do you think you will be all right?'

'I'll be fine,' she said, even though she felt a little bit nervous. 'I will go to the Book Room and find a nice picture book to read.'

'Good girl,' her father said.

After they had cleared away the dishes, Mary went to get her book. She found a nice one, with big, bright pictures of wild animals and stories about each one, and she and Spindle went to one of their favourite parts of the big house to read it: a room full of cosy, squashy chairs and beanbags, and a big window to look out of.

They were reading a story all about a lion who had got caught in a net, and how a little mouse had come along and saved him by nibbling the cords with his sharp teeth (Spindle thought it was the best story he had ever read), when they heard footsteps coming down the hall. Mary thought that perhaps her dad had decided to come and join them after all, and she hopped out of the chair to call him.

But it wasn't her dad. Standing in the doorway, looking into the room, was Marcus.

'Hello, Mary,' he said. 'I think we need to have a little talk.'

Mary found that she could not speak. Her mouth had gone all dry. She just shook her head.

'We had a secret, and you told,' Marcus said, looking sad. 'I thought we were friends.'

'You hurt me,' Mary managed to say at last. 'Friends don't hurt each other.'

Marcus slowly came into the room. Mary tried to back away from him, but she bumped into the chair and couldn't go any further.

'If I hurt you, I'm sorry,' Marcus said. 'I just wanted to show you my favourite game. Maybe I went too fast. Why don't we play again, and you'll see what fun it can be?'

'No!' Mary said, and began to cry.

And she kept saying no, but Marcus made her play anyway.

Jason was very tense beside me.

'He a bad, bad man,' he said, his voice heavy with emotion.

'He's done some bad things,' I agreed. 'What should Mary do now, d'you think?'

168

Jason thought about that. 'She need to tell someone,' he said after a long period of pondering the dilemma.

'Who, though?'

That was a tough one. Jason screwed up his little-old-man's face and puffed and blew as if he might expire any minute. Finally, he looked at me with concern writ large across his features. 'Spindle,' he said. 'She only got Spindle.'

I nodded. 'But Spindle already knows,' I pointed out.

'Oh yeah,' Jason said, slapping his forehead dramatically.

'Will we see what happens?'

He nodded.

Mary didn't bother to tell her dad this time. Spindle begged her to, but she said that there was really no point. She remembered how he had looked when she told him, of how his voice had become all hoarse and how he had clenched his fists. Mary did not want to see him like that; anyway, he had not believed her then – why would he believe her now?

Marcus started eating with them again, and during the day he wanted to play his other, better games with her, and got angry if she said no. Some nights, he came to her bedroom, too. It got so that he seemed to be everywhere she went, and she felt like there was no escape.

Mary began to wonder if it was all her fault. Had she done something to make Marcus think she wanted him to do these things? She thought back over all the days they had spent together; all the conversations they'd had; but she could see not one thing that could have made him wish to hurt her.

'You did nothing wrong, Mary,' Spindle whispered in her ear during the dark hours of the night. 'What Marcus is doing is wrong.'

'But why is he nice to me all the rest of the time?' Mary

asked. 'Sometimes he seems to be such a lovely person, and I like him so much. But then he wants to play the bad games, and I hate him all over again.'

'I do not know, Mary,' Spindle said. 'But I tell you this: if you do not tell your father, I will.'

'Daddy does not like mice,' Mary said. 'He does not hear you when you speak, like I do.'

'I will make him understand,' Spindle said. 'You are my best friend.'

'Perhaps he will not hurt me again,' Mary said. 'He has not in a few days, now.'

And they fell asleep, with Spindle lying beside her on her pillow.

But later, as it was growing bright outside, she woke up, and Marcus was in her room, and she knew that it would never stop. Spindle whispered so only she could hear: 'Be strong, Mary, I am going to your father,' and he shot off the end of her bed and out the door.

'Spindle gonna tell!' Jason said triumphantly.

'What do you think of that?'

'Her daddy not b'lieve her afore.'

'Does that mean he won't believe now?'

Jason chewed his lowed lip furiously. 'Him might b'lieve now,' he said.

'Remember what I said? You tell, and you keep telling until somebody believes you. Mary only has her dad, but he hasn't really done anything mean to her. He's just not a very brave man, and he wanted to think the best of his little brother.'

'That brother was mean!'

'He was, and you know, grown-ups should always put their children first, and take care of them. But sometimes, they don't. Mary's dad hasn't been a very good dad – but maybe he deserves a second chance.'

Jason didn't seem convinced, but I read the next part anyway.

Marcus was long gone when her father came to her. Mary had wrapped herself up tight in the bedclothes and was lying very still. She heard him come in, and his footsteps as he walked across the floor. He sat down on her bed and placed his hand on her shoulder, but Mary felt so awfully sad and cold inside, that she could not bear to look at him. He sat there for a while before he spoke.

'She seems all right to me, mouse,' he said. 'Look, she is asleep.'

Mary could not hear what Spindle said.

'He is my brother, mouse. How can I believe these things you say? I knew him when he was a baby. I protected him from bullies in the schoolyard and picked him up when he fell and cut his knees.'

Again, there was a pause while her friend spoke.

'You are right. She is my little girl.' And now Mary thought she heard tears in her father's voice. 'I will speak to Marcus.'

And then his weight was gone from the bed, and he left her room.

'He gonna speak to Marcus?'

'That's what he says.'

'He should box him in the head.'

Jason demonstrated by throwing a pretty determined right hook into the air and making a yelp Bruce Lee would have been proud to own.

'Maybe he will.'

Jason seemed happy with this thought. 'Adults

shouldn't do them things to childrens,' he said firmly.

'They shouldn't,' I agreed.

'It hurts childrens bad when them things happen.'

'Does it?' I asked, my heart beating a little faster.

He nodded. 'It hurtses here' – he touched his bottom – 'and here' – he touched his groin – 'and here' – his throat.

'Did somebody do that to you, Jase?' I asked.

He nodded.

'Who hurt you, Jason?'

'My daddy,' he said matter-of-factly. 'He hurted me and them other kids.'

I could barely remain sitting down. I wanted to run and get Terri and Sarah, so that someone else could hear what this little boy was disclosing. 'What other kids, Jason?'

He shrugged. 'I dunno,' he said, as if it was a frivolous point. 'All them other kids.'

'Kids you didn't know?'

He nodded. 'Read more.'

The next morning, Mary's dad and Marcus had a terrible argument down in the laboratory. From the breakfast room, she could not hear what they were saying, but she had never heard her father so angry. Spindle was sitting on the table, listening, and although it is very hard to tell with mice, Mary could have sworn he was smiling.

'Let us see how Uncle Marcus feels now,' Spindle said merrily, his long whiskers twitching.

Mary was a bit frightened, but she was also curious to see what would happen. The shouting went on for a very long time, then she heard a creaking as the laboratory door opened, and clattering footsteps on the stairs. Marcus came bursting into the room. He took one look at Spindle sitting on the table, rushed over, and, before the little mouse could move, crushed him with one blow of his fist. Mary could not at first believe what she saw. She blinked, and shook herself, but Spindle's little grey body was still lying on the wooden table-top when she looked again, smashed and broken, and Marcus was wiping a smear of blood off his hand on to his trouser leg. For a second, she was certain that she would faint, but then she started to scream. She screamed and screamed, and could not stop. She thought that she had finally gone mad, and the thought actually made her glad. If I am mad, she said to herself, none of it will matter. Marcus can do what he likes, and I won't care one bit. Her screams brought her father running, and when he saw what Marcus had done, he ran over and grabbed his brother. Mary never found out what happened after that, because it got so that she was screaming so much, she forgot to breathe, and she actually did faint, falling in a heap on to the floor.

'Why'd he kill that mouse Spindle?' Jason asked, obviously very annoyed at this turn of events.

'When bad things happen, we can get hurt in all sorts of ways that make us sad and angry for a very, very long time,' I said.

'That Spindle was a good mouse to have around the place,' Jason said. 'He could talk and everything.'

'Mary was lonely,' I said. 'She needed a friend, didn't she?'

'Who be her friend now?'

'We'll have to see,' I said.

When Mary woke up, her throat was sore and she found that she must have been crying even in her sleep, because her pillow was wet from tears. For a lovely moment, she did not know why she might have been crying in her sleep, and she was going to ask Spindle, but then she remembered, and felt very much like crying all over again. Her dad was asleep in an armchair beside her bed, and for a while she just lay there and watched him. He looked sad and tired and worried, and as he slept he muttered and shifted restlessly. At last, he awoke and saw that she was awake too.

'Mary,' he said. 'Are you all right?'

'Yes, Daddy,' she said. 'Where is Marcus?'

'He is gone,' her dad said. 'Gone from the big house, and he is never coming back again.'

'He killed Spindle,' Mary said, and the tears began to trickle down her cheeks in streams.

'Yes, he did. Spindle was a brave mouse, and a good friend to you. A better friend than I was.'

'Now he is gone.'

'I will try to be your friend, if you will allow me.'

And Mary smiled for the first time in many days. 'I would like that very much, Daddy.'

And so, Mary's dad spent less time in his laboratory, and when he did go down to work on his experiments and mix his powders, Mary went with him, and he taught her all about chemicals and how heat and cold made them do strange and interesting things.

Mary taught him how to play some of the games she liked, and she discovered that Marcus had left his toys behind, and they were just as much fun now that he was gone – after all, it was not their fault that he had done nasty things.

But sometimes, late at night, Mary would wake up from a bad dream, and think for a moment that he had come back, and that he wanted to play, and she could not scream no matter how hard she tried. And she would lie and stare into the dark, frightened to breathe, and stay there until the sun came up. Then, when it was bright, she would run on tip-toe to her father's room and creep under the covers and snuggle down beside him, and he would open one eye and say: 'Need a little company, Mary?' and she would nod her head, and feel safe and warm again for a while.

But on stormy nights, when the thunder boomed and crashed and lightning carved a path across the sky, Mary would sit by her window and gaze out at the mountainside. She would miss Spindle so much it felt like an ache deep inside her, and she would watch to see if there was anyone climbing up the winding road to their front door – watch and hope that there was not.

'That all the story?' Jason asked.

'Yes. That's it, Jase.'

'Her daddy done right for her, at the end.'

'In the end, yes.'

'My daddy, he didn't do right for me.'

I didn't say anything. Jason looked at me with a strange expression – there was something too old about it, a sense that there was nothing I could do or say that he had not heard before.

'My mammy, she never done nothin',' he said. 'My mammy, she like the daddy in that story.'

I hugged him, then, as much for me as for him. The crows outside the window sustained their constant chatter, and in the kitchen down the hallway, I could hear the clatter and clang of plates as Sarah started dinner. The world continued, despite what this waif had just told me, regardless of the foul things he had witnessed and experienced.

'I'm sorry, Jase,' I said. 'I'm sorry that happened to you.'

'Why you sorry? You didn't do nothin',' Jason said, and I hugged him all the tighter.

28

Sarah and I sat in the window of a pub down the road
from The Crow's Nest the following morning, with
Terri, all at sixes and sevens with nerves, seated across
from us.

'You've written up what he said?' Terri asked for the
fifth time.

'I have,' I said. 'I've included a copy of the story I read
him, so they can see we didn't put words in his mouth.
The father isn't even the baddie in it, for God's sake. I've
tried to record every statement he made verbatim, but, to
be honest, I'm not even sure we're going to need it: he's
kind of gone into disclosure overload.'

'What?'

'Well, he told me, and all the other kids, that his "daddy
done bad things", over supper last night,' Sarah said. 'He
then proceeded to act out an example of just what Daddy
done. He's quite a mime.'

'Isn't he, though,' I agreed. 'It took me hours to get
him to bed last night. He wanted the story again, and
this time every other line he was cutting in, telling me
about this, that and the other time he was hurt by his
daddy.'

'And he's consistent in mentioning these other children
his father brought home and abused too?'

'Definitely,' I said. 'There is no question that other
children were involved. He says he didn't know them,
never knew their names, but he is definite that they were

a regular feature of the abuse. He refers to them all the time, now.'

The pub was an early house, dark, quiet and cool at eleven o'clock, with only a couple of regulars seated at the bar.

'You did good, guys,' Terri said. 'This is what we need to get Conor put away for what should be a good while. Incest is one thing, but abduction, blatant predatory paedophilia; well, that's quite another.'

'When is the trial, Terri?' Sarah asked.

'Next week. This may delay things slightly, because the lawyers will have to weave this into their case, and they'll obviously require time to prepare, but since the Benjy incident, this has been on the cards. It's been the elephant in the room, really.'

'So how does Jason fit into it all?' I asked.

'How d'you mean?' Terri said.

'Well, our case is all based on his testimony, isn't it?'

'Yeah,' Terri nodded.

'How's he going to testify?'

'You've never been to family court before?' Terri asked me.

'No,' I admitted.

'Me neither,' Sarah piped up.

'Well, it could go one of two ways,' Terri said. 'Ideally, Jason would speak to the court in camera. You know what that means?'

Terri was referring to instances where children could give evidence in private – the counsels for each side of the case, and the judge, would be present while Jason gave evidence, but cross-examination would be kept to a bare minimum.

'He's so young,' Sarah said. 'It doesn't seem right.'

'I know,' Terri agreed. 'In Oz they use video link-ups, which are less stressful for the child, but that isn't done in Ireland.'

'And what if he freezes up, or doesn't want to talk that day?' I asked.

'We can use the statements he's made – your report, in other words – as testimony,' Terri said. 'It's less impressive, but I think it might be enough.'

'It should be,' Sarah said, annoyed. 'Children of Jason's age don't make up stuff like this!'

Terri smiled. 'But they do get things confused,' she said. 'What if Conor had had porno movies playing in the house, and Jason saw some of them? What if Mark had told him about the abuse he experienced, and Jason got it all mixed up in his head? What if Conor Farrell really is a genuine, decent bloke who truly was trying to bring young Benjy back to his parents, and Jase's words, based on a big mistake, put him in prison?'

'But that isn't the case,' Sarah said.

'And the courts have to make sure,' Terri said. 'Understand?'

'I understand,' I said. 'But I don't like it. Not one bit.'

'Well, that's all right, matey,' Terri said. 'I don't like it much either. But it's a part of what we do, so let's just grin and bear it, and present a united front for the children. I know this doesn't directly affect Ellen, Mark and Leo, but they'll all sense that something's going on. We need to keep the day-to-day stuff as normal as possible, all right?'

Sarah and I nodded.

'And there's one more thing,' Terri said. 'And you need to prepare yourselves for it. We all do.'

'What?'

'Timmy, the older brother has started talking about what went on at home, too.'

Sarah and I exchanged a surprised look. 'And?' I said.

'It largely corroborates what Jason has said.'

'How long have you known about this?' I asked.

'A little while.'

'And you didn't think it was something we needed to know?'

'I knew you'd be pissed off,' Terri said, 'but it was crucial you got the facts independently. If I fed you full of what Timmy had been saying, there was always the possibility you'd somehow, subliminally, even, steer Jason in the same direction – leading questions and whatnot.'

'Well, if Timmy is saying the same thing, surely this is an open-and-shut case,' Sarah said.

'Well, quite,' Terri said. 'But see, he's also more or less cleared his mum.'

'So?'

'Her lawyers are looking to have Jason prepared for a move home if Conor goes to prison.'

'I don't follow,' I said.

'If Conor Farrell goes down,' Terri said, leaning forward for emphasis, 'Jason will, more than likely, go back home.'

29

It was early on a Saturday morning, and Jason and I were in the playground. He was, by now, a veteran user of the swings and the roundabout, but the slide continued to elude him. I had attempted just about every method I could think of to entice him to the top of that ladder, but nothing seemed to work. I thought it was a pity, but reasoned that he'd get there in time, and decided not to force the issue.

This particular morning the area was deserted as usual. I was sitting on a bench, watching Jason swing idly back and forth, my mind fixed on the approaching court case, when I realized another child was standing on the perimeter of the play area. I recognized the youngster as a neighbour, a young boy of six or seven who lived a short distance down the road. I looked over to Jason, and saw that he was watching the new arrival with suspicion. I wondered what he would do. The Jason of even six weeks ago would have either jumped from the swing and run off, or attacked the intruder. As the older child walked over to us, I realized that, perhaps for the first time since coming to The Crow's Nest, Jason was uncertain how to react.

The newcomer stood just a few feet away for a moment, then got on to the swing right next to Jason. Together, without saying a word, the two boys swung side by side. Generally, they moved with their eyes forward, watching the horizon as it soared and fell in accordance with their movements, but occasionally one would cast a surreptitious glance at the other.

I knew that the interloper was well aware who Jason was – a group of 'orphans' (as our children were locally known) did not move into such a comfortable, well-established area without attracting quite a bit of fascinated attention. I assumed curiosity had got the better of the fear this boy must have naturally felt, and prompted him to see what all the fuss was about.

After five minutes of swinging, both boys slowed, pacing one another perfectly, and finally came to a halt. The new arrival hopped to the ground, and ran directly over to the slide, which he climbed frenetically, standing at the top, waiting for Jason to follow him. Jason, however, had other ideas, and simply stayed on the ground, looking dejected. *Here we go*, I thought, barely daring to breathe while all this unfolded. *It'll kick off nicely, now.* I genuinely expected Jason to wait for his newfound friend to slide to ground level, and then attempt to bludgeon him to a pulp.

Down came the boy. Jason walked slowly to the end of the slide's chute. I stood, ready to intercede if violence erupted. Yet the altercation never happened.

'What's the matter?'

Jason looked at the other boy without answering.

'Don'tcha like the slide?'

Jason shook his head.

'Why not?'

Go on, Jase, I thought. *Talk to him!*

'I don't like the ladder thing,' Jason finally said, so quietly I could barely hear from where I sat.

'C'mon, I'll teach ya,' came the reply.

The duo walked around the slide in a wide arc, as if to

181

better see it from all angles. Then they sat for a while in complete silence, but I was aware that there was quite a bit of non-verbal communication going on. Eventually, the new boy stood up and climbed the ladder, his eye on Jason the whole time. When he reached the top he stopped and looked down at his friend firmly but with sympathy. 'Look at me,' he said, and slid down. He did it quite slowly, using his hands to stop himself twice, showing that the descent could be easily controlled. Then he walked over to Jason and took his reluctant student by the hand.

'I used to be scared too,' he said. 'Come on.'

Jason allowed himself to be led to the slide. His friend pushed him gently to the front. Jason climbed up the ladder slowly, his cohort a step or two below, every now and again glancing at where I was sitting close by. At the top, he held tightly on to the rail and looked back at his companion, who was standing directly behind him.

'Go on!' the bigger boy said, gently pushing him into a sitting position. I watched this gentle manhandling nervously. Jason was not used to being treated in such a way – the other children at The Crow's Nest always kept him at arm's length, and the only physical contact he ever received from the staff was to be hugged or cuddled. Yet Jason bore the touch from his mentor with goodwill, and was pushed slowly over the edge.

He slid down painfully slowly, stopping himself with his hands every now and then as he had seen demonstrated, laughing nervously all the way. When he reached the bottom he let out a victory whoop and ran over to me, giving me a hug and telling me in a great rush of words how he had been scared, but he did it anyway. The other little boy looked over at us, grinned to himself, and wandered away. He had accomplished in one simple act of gentle friendship what I had been trying to do for months. Before he could get far, Jason was after him.

'Hey, fella,' he called. 'What's your name?'

'Albert.'

'Wanna play on that slide thing with me some more?'

'Yeah, 'kay.'

'C'mon, then, Albert, let's go play. Did you see me, Albert, how I slided down, even though I was scared? You taught me how to do that, di'n'tcha, Albert?'

I realized as I watched the pair run back to the slide that I was crying, and had no idea why. Maybe it was because, in a beautiful moment of innocent camaraderie, Jason Farrell had done something very brave: he had taken a chance on the kindness of a stranger. Suddenly, he didn't seem so lost and lonely any more.

30

The children were all in bed, the daily logs and reports were written and the house was quiet. Sarah and I sat in the living room, watching *The Searchers*.

'You know, I can't work out whether or not I think John Wayne is good-looking,' Sarah said sleepily.

'Probably not by today's standards,' I said. 'I mean, put him beside Keanu Reeves or Mel Gibson, and he looks pretty ropy. Ideas about that sort of thing change all the time. Somebody said once that Humphrey Bogart had a face only a mother could love, but in the forties and fifties, he was considered quite the matinee idol.'

'Who do you like, then?' Sarah asked, stretching out on the couch.

'Movie stars and such?'

'Yeah.'

'I dunno. Used to have quite the thing for Julia Roberts. It was unrequited, though. She never calls, she never writes. I am doomed to worship from afar.'

'Poor you.'

'What about you?'

'Oohh ... I love Mickey Rourke. Did you see *Angel Heart*?'

'I did. Great movie,' I said. 'You like the bad boys, obviously.'

'Always. It is not a habit that has served me well.'

'I can imagine. You probably won't find too many rough and ready types in social care, either.'

'No,' Sarah agreed. 'Trainee priests and homosexuals.'

'That is a gross generalization.'

'I know. But it's not totally untrue, either.'

'So why'd you get involved in this type of work, then?'

'Process of elimination,' Sarah said. 'I'm crap at maths, useless with money, but good with people. I'm not smart enough to be a doctor, too clumsy to be an air hostess, and faint when I see blood, so nursing was out. That left childcare.'

'I think you're selling yourself short,' I said.

'What about you?'

'Well, if you don't count the fact that I'm also crap at maths, useless with money, can't stand the sight of blood . . .'

'You did fine when Jason cut Yolanda!'

'I was fainting inside.'

'I don't think I believe you,' Sarah said, reaching over and punching me gently on the arm. 'Come on. How'd you end up here?'

'Childcare sort of crept up on me as a career,' I said, unsure how I was going to answer the question. I had never really thought about it deeply before – it just seemed better to me than working in a factory or a super-market. 'I still sometimes find myself surprised that this is what I wound up doing. Looking back, I suppose I can trace the first inklings to a camping trip when I was maybe eleven or twelve.'

'You don't strike me as the outdoorsy type.'

'I'm not,' I concurred, 'but my parents were. We'd gone to the beach, and were sitting around outside the tent after lunch one afternoon. The only newspaper that ever really came into our house when I was a kid was the *Daily Mail*, and on the afternoon in question I was lounging about in the sun in our little campsite in the dunes, reading the odd article.'

'As you do,' Sarah agreed.

'I came across one that involved a three-year-old boy who had been murdered by his stepfather. The man had been prosecuted, but during the trial details of most appalling abuse had come to light. I can clearly recall a sense of . . . rage, I suppose it must have been, as I read, and an underlying feeling of being disturbed by it. This would have been 1983, and child abuse was still a very underground thing back then. I didn't even know that was what it was called. But I knew it was terribly wrong, and that someone should have stopped it.'

'So you were an idealist, even then,' Sarah said, smiling.

'I guess,' I said. 'You know what's funny?'

'What?'

'I can't even remember that child's name, now. But I do remember thinking that there should have been someone there to help him; somebody should have stopped that awful man from hurting and ultimately killing that child. And I thought, at that moment, that it would not be such a bad thing to do for a job. Back then, I had never even heard of social workers, and childcare workers were even further from my mind – I envisioned a police officer dedicated to protecting children. But that thought very definitely popped into my mind.'

'You were only a kid yourself,' Sarah said. 'You thought in absolutes. Probably saw yourself abseiling down the side of a block of flats, bursting in through a window to carry the little boy to safety.'

'Something like that.'

'So, was that enough to send you looking for childcare courses?'

'No. It probably came back to me as an idea when I was around fourteen. I was walking home one evening from school when, up ahead of me, I noticed someone – John, a guy I knew, probably five or six years older than me, who had Down's Syndrome. I knew John quite well – he lived just down the road from me – but it was a warm evening, and I didn't speed my pace to catch up with him. I just wandered on caught up in my own thoughts.'

'Something tells me the story doesn't end there, though,' Sarah said.

'No. I was moseying on, minding my own business, when I heard someone calling John names, and when I looked up, there was a group of kids around him. I knew them all. Some were from my school, some from near where I lived. Before more than a minute had passed, they began to throw stones at him, too.'

'What did you do?' Sarah asked.

'I was shocked and sickened by what I was seeing, and I very much wanted to rush up and tell them to leave him alone. What I remember more than anything else is the dignity with which he continued walking, while the stones bounced about his feet, or even hit him. He never broke into a run, just held his head high and continued to make his way home. I recall thinking that he was probably used to being bullied and ridiculed. It didn't make it any easier for me to watch, but neither did it cause me to actually go to his defence.'

'You didn't do anything?' Sarah said gently. It wasn't an accusation, just a statement.

'No. I did not even call out to them to stop,' I said. I had never articulated this to anyone before, and it didn't feel good to do so now. But Sarah and I had pledged

187

honesty. 'Despite my righteous anger at the plight of that little boy in the newspaper column, when life placed someone in need of protection right under my nose, I failed the test. I continued to hang back and feel impotently angry. They followed him for some distance, tormenting and mocking him. And I never said a word or lifted a finger to stop them.'

'Being a teenager sucks,' Sarah said. 'No one wants to stick their neck out. You want to blend in, to be one of the crowd, even if that means something shitty.'

'Not good enough,' I said. 'To this day I have been ashamed of my cowardice, because cowardice is exactly what caused me to stay silent. But after that experience, I swore never to keep quiet again.'

'So was that the Road to Damascus moment?'

'No, I think that happened two years later, when I was sixteen, in a band, and dead-set on becoming the next Bono.'

'You wanted to be Bono?' Sarah said with disdain

'There weren't many Irish alternatives,' I said. 'Anyway, they made some really good music in the eighties. *The Unforgettable Fire* is a stormer of an album. I know *The Joshua Tree* is overrated, but come on . . .'

'Jesus, Shane, don't be so insular. You could have opted for Bob Dylan, or Neil Young, or even Mike Scott.'

'I did like Mike Scott, but I won't pretend that my musical tastes extended to Dylan when I was sixteen. I was cool, but I wasn't that cool.'

'All right, but is this going to take much longer? I would like to get to bed sometime tonight.'

'No, we're nearly there. And you did ask.'

'I didn't expect you were going to be giving your entire life's story.'

'Shut up and listen,' I said. 'My mother was teaching in a school for children with intellectual disabilities. She had been pestering me, as only mothers can, to come down and play some songs for the children, as it was coming close to Christmas.'

'Ah, carol singing. You went, I take it?'

'Well, eventually. I had been putting her off for a while, but she was determined to have her way, and eventually I gave in. Guitar in hand, I headed down to the school to get it over with. And, to my utmost surprise, I ended up having a wonderful time.'

'Of course you did.'

'These children – the class she was teaching were mostly seven or eight years old – didn't care what I looked like. They didn't care where I came from or which step on the ladder of social class I was on. All they were interested in was the fact that I had come to spend time with them.'

'And you were hooked.'

'It was a moment of pure, undiluted honesty,' I admitted. 'I walked home realizing that, in the unlikely event that my rock career didn't take off, working with kids wasn't such a bad back-up plan.'

'So, despite your initial honourable intentions, your eventual reasons were fairly selfish.'

I looked at her in feigned disgust.

'You've hurt my feelings now.'

'I doubt that,' Sarah said. 'I know for a fact that your ludicrous sense of honour and justice is fully intact. Rock music's loss is our gain. Now' – she stretched and yawned – 'if you are quite finished, I'm going to get a bit of sleep before the first late-night wake-up call. I'll see you in the morning.'

'I think I'll watch the end of the movie.'

'Haven't you seen it before?'

'Only around fifteen times.'

'He finds her, I take it.'

'He found her twenty minutes ago.'

'Oh. I must have missed that. I'm off.'

'Yeah, night, Sarah.'

Despite the best intentions, I nodded off myself, and woke with a start to see the Duke striding away from the front door of the Jorgensens' cabin, alone and stoic against a stark skyline. I didn't know what had woken me, and, switching off the television, I went into the kitchen to get a glass of water. I was standing at the sink, drinking it, when I heard movement and what sounded like a muffled cry from the hallway.

I put the glass down quickly and went out to see which of the children was up. The corridor proved to be empty, but in my peripheral vision I saw someone move past the door of the living room.

'Forget something?' I called, sure it was Sarah coming back down to get her shoes or a cardigan or some item she had jettisoned. When no answer came, I walked the few steps to the door.

A figure stood at the end of the room, in the shadows behind the couch. For a moment I couldn't tell who it was, but then a cloud moved from in front of the moon, and I saw her standing in an old-fashioned red dress, her hair pulled tight against her scalp in the fashion of the time. I can tell you that she was a little over five feet tall, very slender and impossibly pale. I can say for certain that the bodice of her dress was beaded intricately, and that her feet were delicate and tiny. Of her face, I can recall nothing. I know it had a look of deep sadness etched upon it, and that her eyes were dark, almost black.

I am sure her make-up was expertly applied and that, despite what I had said to Sarah earlier about ideas of what is or is not good-looking changing, she would be considered very beautiful regardless of the tastes of the era she found herself in. But somehow, her features seemed to be moving, running together as I looked, so that for a moment I had a sense of dizziness and nausea, as if I was seeing her from a great height.

Then, in a blink, I was alone in the room, and she was gone. All that remained was the light of a new moon, and a sense of loss.

NOW

31

Jason Farrell was wearing a suit I had just purchased for him, and looked uncomfortable and irritable in it.

'I've got a lovely tracksuit that I only wore the one time,' he said. 'Why can't I wear that to court?'

'Because the judge is going to be seeing quite a number of people tomorrow, and the vast majority of them will be dressed in tracksuits,' I said, patiently. 'You'll stand out as different.'

'And I want to do that, do I?'

'You do,' I said. 'You want him to see that you care about what you've done, and that you are prepared to make an effort to change.'

'That don't mean I want to start dressin' like a prick.'

'You don't look like a prick,' I said, truthfully. 'You look like someone who doesn't often wear a suit. You'll get used to it.'

'Will you be dressed like this too?'

'I will,' I said. 'Look, you know I'm not one for formalities and the like, and I'm usually a scruffy bastard, but when you go to court, even to read a report or give evidence, you're expected to show respect. I don't much like lawyers and your experience with them has probably been pretty negative, but we all need to deal with them from time to time.'

'What's the judge like?'

'You're probably going to be seen by Harriet Muldoon. She's tough, but she's fair.'

'A woman judge? Is the real one on holidays or some-thin'?'

'A lot of judges are women now, Jason,' I said wearily. 'And if you start giving her a hard time, she will send you down so far we'll need shovels to dig you out.'

Jason snorted in laughter. 'Relax, man. I'll be on me best behaviour.'

'That does not make me feel one bit better.'

Jason laughed again. We were in his room at Phelim's. He still had most of his clothes and odds and ends in plastic bags scattered here and there about the place, as if he was sending a clear message to me and the world that this was a temporary arrangement – he was not going to remain there under any circumstances.

'Are you clear on what you're going to say, Jase? When the judge asks you?'

'Yeah – I'm gonna ask her out on a date.'

I put my head in my hands. 'Jason, I swear to you, if you pull any crap during this hearing, there will be nothing I can do for you. The reason you're here in the first place is because your attitude to women and children is so poor. If you start pulling some kind of sexist bullshit on Judge Muldoon, you can hardly blame her for getting tough on you.'

'Maybe I'd like her to get tough on me – have you thought of that?' Jason said lecherously.

'That's enough, Jason,' I said, starting to get genuinely annoyed with him. 'I really wonder sometimes if you want to get your life sorted out at all. You certainly don't seem to today.'

'Aw, come on now,' Jason said, watching me from the mirror he'd been looking at his besuited appearance in. 'I'm only messin' about. When I'm asked to talk to the judge, I'll tell her I know what I done was wrong, and I'll say sorry.'

'And what do you call her?'

'Your worship?'

I laughed, this time. 'No, that's a bishop, I think. Just call her Judge. That'll be fine.'

'What if she asks me hard stuff?'

'She won't. They'll be seeing all kinds of cases tomorrow, and they generally move through them fairly quickly. We've made a suggestion as to how you should be treated, and they're seeing you before your seventeenth birthday, which is a good sign. Your mum will be there to say she's going to be available to you during the programme, and that she'll support you afterwards – I think this'll go swimmingly.'

'I fuckin' hope so.'

'Me too.'

Jason fiddled with his tie. He looked young and skinny and frail. The past few weeks had taken their toll on him.

'Jase?'

'What?'

'You really do know what you did was wrong, don't you?'

He turned to look at me. 'Why are you askin' me that?'

'Because it's important to me,' I said. 'I need to know this is real, not just you trying to get out of going to jail.'

For a moment I thought he was going to hit me. I prepared to slide out of the way, but then he threw his arms about my neck, and held me tightly. 'I know what I done to that old woman and them kids was bad. I know that, Shane,' he said. 'And I want to put it right. I swear I do.'

I hugged him back. 'I'm glad of that, Jason,' I said. 'If you want this to work, then I know it will.'

I only realized several days later what a stupid thing to say that was.

32

Judge Harriet Muldoon entered the room as if she owned it, which was not strictly true, but felt as if it was. She was a tall, thin woman in her late fifties, and spoke with an educated Anglo-Irish accent. If I hadn't known that she dealt with countless young men like Jason Farrell every day, I might have been concerned that he was on to a loser straight away. As it was, I had other things on my mind.

'Where's me ma?' Jason had asked, panic etched across his face, when we arrived at the court.

I searched the room anxiously. There was no sign of her.

'She probably got caught in the traffic,' I said, not very convinced by my own excuse.

'She doesn't like courts,' Jason said. 'Too many Gardaí about.'

'She'll be here,' I said.

As we sat waiting, a short, pudgy man led a frail old woman up the central aisle of the room. Jason nudged me with his elbow, and nodded in her direction.

'That's her,' he hissed.

'Who?'

'The old woman I did over.'

I immediately wished I could shrink into the seat and disappear. The old lady and her escort sat almost directly across from us. If she noticed Jason, she made no show of it, simply gazing ahead at the podium where the judge would shortly be seated. I looked at her surreptitiously from the corner of my eye. Marks of violence were still visible on her face, and I did not know if the stick she used was a recent addition, or another result of Jason's tender mercies.

What must she think of me, I wondered, sitting here with the monster who had so ill-treated her. I was used to being in the company of the victims, of standing firm with them against those who would oppress the weak and the defenceless. Taking the side of the abuser was a new experience for me. I did not like it one bit.

Liz Farrell never showed up. Thankfully, the judge seemed prepared to let it slide – this time.

Kris Isaacson was another man entirely when in the courtroom. His entire posture was different, he spoke without that odd accent, and, even though I know it doesn't make sense, he actually seemed much slimmer when standing and addressing the judge. I looked on in wonderment – could this be the same lethargic, mono-syllabic man I had met in St Phelim's conference room?

'Judge, my client is cooperating fully with the staff at the remand and assessment unit where he is now residing, and is also in close contact with a support worker from the Dunleavy Trust, a worker whom he actively sought out in an attempt to finally come to terms with the magnitude and pathology of his problems,' Isaacson said.

Well, that's not strictly true, I thought. *But it sounds good.*

I looked over, and saw that the old woman was now staring intently at us. I squirmed. She had a hard, cold gaze. Jason seemed utterly oblivious to it.

'In conjunction with the therapeutic approach at St Phelim's it has been proposed that Jason Farrell participate in a group counselling programme to address the issues of sexual abuse he experienced at the hands of his father, and the subsequent nature of his own offences, which are obviously part of a cycle – a cry for help, if you will,' Isaacson said, his voice booming and theatrical.

'He's been in these programmes before,' Judge Harriet Muldoon said. 'What's different now?'

'My client is currently sixteen years old. Age and experience have taught him remorse, and he is also aware that a lifetime in an adult prison looms large if he does not go about altering his patterns of behaviour.'

'That all sounds well and good, Mr Isaacson,' the judge said, flicking through the pages in Jason's file. 'But these are extremely well-established behaviour patterns. There are two sexual assaults in this young man's past, a firearms offence, he is a known associate of criminals and thugs – I'm inclined to send him down for a term, see how that sits with him.'

'Can he at least have a chance to state his case, Judge?'

'I'll hear him,' Harriet Muldoon said, sitting back.

Isaacson motioned at Jason, who stood, quivering from head to toe.

'Mr Farrell, you stand before me a changed man, according to your solicitor,' the judge said. 'Why should I believe you are any different now?'

Jason said not a word, just gazed at the judge, his hands clutched before him, his mouth slack.

'Mr Farrell, my time and the time of this court is precious. Do you have anything to say for yourself?'

'I . . . I'm sorry for what I done,' Jason said in trembling tones. 'I know I hurted that woman.' He nodded towards his victim, who continued to stare us down. 'I know that was a bad, bad thing. I wants to show people that I can do good. I don't want to be a bad person no more. They tells me that this programme could help me to stop doin' the wrong stuff all the time. They're ... they're gonna teach me how to make good choices.'

The judge narrowed her eyes, and looked at the skinny, shivering individual. 'And you will make every effort to facilitate this programme in any way you can?'

'Yes, Judge.'

'And I see your mother is going to take you home again, and will vouch for you?'

I froze.

'Yes, Judge.'

She sighed. 'Very well. I am releasing you into the care of the staff at St Phelim's Remand and Assessment Unit. You will participate in the programme as outlined, and I will see you here in four months, with the psychologist from that programme, to establish how fit you are to return home.'

Jason beamed from ear to ear.

'But I want you to pay close attention to me, Mr Farrell. If the conditions I have just laid out are not met, if you show yourself to be unworthy of the chance I am giving you, I will have no option but to give you a custodial sentence, which will see you going to Salt Island before very long, and you do not want that, take my word for it. Do you understand?'

'I do, Judge.'

'So be it. You can go.'

Isaacson nodded at me, and Jason and I stood up to go. The eyes of the old woman remained on us all the way out. Jason was walking on air – I felt as if I might be sick.

33

At nine o'clock that night, I sat in my office in Dunleavy House, smoking a cigarette and looking out the window at the overgrown, wild garden that Ben Tyrrell allowed to grow in the courtyard. I never knew why he allowed the trees, shrubs and bushes to run riot the way he did. I had asked him once, and he had just shrugged and said: 'Why not?'

I never asked again.

It was dark and raining heavily. I was tired and hungry, but couldn't face going home. A music session was set to start at ten in The Minstrel Boy, and I knew Ben sometimes played there, so I thought I might go over. But I was still angry with my boss. I felt he had abandoned me, and wasn't sure if I wanted to be around him. That said, I was confused and worn out with this case, and needed some guidance.

I heard the front door open and close. One of the other staff must be working late, too, I thought. After a few moments the door to my office opened, and Beverly Munro came in. I took my feet down from the desk and stood to meet her.

'What are you doing here?' I asked. 'You're supposed to be taking some time off.'

'I saw the light on,' she said, sitting in Loretta's chair opposite me. 'Old habits die hard, I suppose.'

I sat back down, too. 'Do you want some coffee?'

'No, thank you. Have you spoken to Ben, Shane?'

I sighed. 'I was thinking about it. Thought I might go over to the session in The Minstrel this evening.'

'He won't be there,' Mrs Munro said. 'He's kind of like a hermit, just at the moment. He's going through a rough time.'

'Aren't we all?' I said.

'Shane, he's given his life to this work, this thing you all do. He's had everything he believes in exploded in front of his eyes. It's been horrible for him.'

'I don't know that running away was the best way of dealing with that,' I said. 'He always taught me to stand and face whatever demons you had. I've lived a good deal of my life by the wisdom of the great Ben Tyrrell. Now it looks like he can't even practise what he preaches.'

'He's not some kind of guru, Shane,' Beverly said gently.

'You could have fooled me!'

'Shane, Ben is the type of person others tend to project their own needs on to. I don't know if you have some sort of father issues, or a need for approval, but you have always placed him on a pedestal and expected a level of perfection that is just impossible for anyone to achieve. Give him a break – he's given you enough, over the years.'

'He didn't seem too keen on giving Jason Farrell a break.'

Mrs Munro threw her eyes to heaven.

'What is it with that boy? I've seen you walk away from cases before. You're realistic. Why can't you let him go?'

'We're in the business of helping people, Mrs Munro. That's all I'm trying to do.'

'Why?'

I blinked at that. 'How do you mean?'

'Why are you going out of your way to help *this* boy? All good sense would suggest that there are others better qualified to deal with his needs. I know you have some warped sense of duty, or need, but it's just you and me here, Shane. What's the real reason?'

'This is what we do,' I stammered. 'He's lost – he's made mistakes . . .'

She continued, doggedly. She could be a tough woman, when she wanted to be, and I was no match for her.

'Do you have some sense you let him down, in the past? Is this about some kind of personal, unfinished business? Are you angry with yourself, rather than Ben? Or is it that Ben is doing to you what you felt you did to Jason Farrell, all those years ago? Is he projecting some-thing on to you you'd rather not see?'

'I didn't let him down,' I almost shouted. 'It was his mother!'

Beverly Munro nodded, sagely. 'But you felt to blame.'

'No. That's not true.'

She stood up. 'Think about it, Shane. Ben's reaction to this was real. One thing you have to give Ben Tyrrell, he's completely honest, with everyone else as well as himself. I'm not sure the same can be said about you – not in this case, at least.'

She walked out, leaving me fuming and hurting. It was another two hours before I could bring myself to go home – being alone with myself in my apartment was more than I could bear.

THEN

34

Albert and Jason were playing in the back garden of The Crow's Nest, kicking a ball back and forth, each of them making great, exaggerated dives and lunges to catch the ball when it came near them, even if they didn't need to move particularly far. I watched them from the window of the kitchen, amazed at children's capacity to continuously find joy in simple things, regardless of what else was going on about them.

The court case against Jason's father was in its second day. I had already given my report, outlining the disclosures Jason had made, and also describing my meeting with Conor and the little boy he had 'found'.

This was all well and good, but Conor had produced an ace from up his sleeve that none of us had expected: an absolutely brilliant lawyer. His name was Brian Utley. He was young, full of piss and vinegar, and was doggedly determined to get Conor as lenient a sentence as he possibly could. How he was paying for the solicitor, none of us knew, but by the end of that first day, I had even found myself feeling sorry for Conor. Utley had presented a detailed account of Farrell's own childhood, complete with an almost pornographic description of the abuses he had had to endure at the hands of his own violent father and uncle.

None of this detail surprised me – my training had taught me that the vast majority of abusers were themselves molested, but to listen to the details, and to see

Farrell sitting at the top of the room, his head bowed, clean-shaven, dressed in a suit that probably cost more than I earned in a month, it was all too easy to forget that this was someone who had done awful things, and was a risk to society. The child Gearoid, whom Conor had called Benjy, had still not uttered a single word since being found by the police, and a psychologist with the Health Board suggested to the court that this might be because Conor had expressly told him 'not to say anything', an instruction which, if backed up with enough fear, might indeed inspire a child to remain silent indefinitely.

Utley had, of course, countered this by pointing out that such a speculation was just that, a speculation, and based on nothing but guesswork. The judge, a grey-haired man with a florid face and an ample girth hidden beneath his black robes, had disregarded this comment, stating that any speculative comments from the psych-ologist were based on years of professional experience with disturbed children, and that he had been asked to address the court as an expert witness.

I felt that doubt had already been introduced, however, and was left with a genuine sense of discomfort. This was not going as easily as it should.

Jason was aware of the case, but we all felt he was too young to truly grasp the full nature of what it meant. Sarah and I had taken him for a walk by the River Torc on the first day of the trial, and I had explained to him that his father was speaking to a judge about what he had done, and that he would have to make amends for his actions. Sarah had added that it was agreed by every-one that hurting children was wrong, and that everyone deserved to be warm and safe, have enough to eat and drink, and be happy. Jason listened to all this gravely, and asked what might happen to his daddy if the judge got really cross with him.

'He gonna shout at him?' Jason wanted to know.

'No, he won't shout,' I said. 'There are really strict rules in the court about what people can and can't do. You have to be polite to one another.'

'So the judge won't give out to him?' Jason said, his tone expressing that he was now wondering what the point of it all was.

'No, he will probably give out, all right, and when this is all finished, your daddy will most likely have to go to prison for a while, to learn how not to hurt kids again.'

Jason considered this. 'What prison like?'

I looked to Sarah for help, but she just kind of shrugged.

'It's a big building, with lots of rooms where people live and sleep, and you can work, and go to classes – you're just not allowed to go home until the judge decides you've learned enough. They lock the doors, and watch to make sure nobody escapes.'

'He be scared?'

'Yeah, some people are afraid when they go there first, but they get used to it.'

'Will he have his dinner in prison?'

'Of course,' I said. 'I think the food is quite good, actually.'

Jason sighed deeply. 'Him be mad about this. Him not gonna want to go in there.'

'He won't have any choice, Jase,' Sarah said. 'The police will make him go, and he'll just have to like it.'

'I see him?' Jason said.

'Maybe when the case is over,' I said.

'I see my mammy?'

'I'll set it up,' I said. Liz had been the least reliable family member at the access visits. It was very hit and miss whether she would turn up any day or not, regardless of any arrangements made.

Jason seemed happy with this, and we sang 'Old MacDonald' all the way back to the car.

So I sat at the kitchen window, and watched Jason playing with his new friend Albert. Here was a child who was gradually finding his own self amid a tangle of darkness and fear. I fervently hoped that nothing would happen to set that search back.

I was on my way out the door to a gig that evening, my coat and scarf on, my banjo in my hand and my guitar slung across my back, when the phone rang.

'Shane, it's Terri. I need to talk to you.'

'Okay, shoot.'

'No – this isn't the kind of conversation we can have over the phone. I need to meet you.'

'I'm going out, Terri. I'm playing music this evening.'

'Is it anything you can cancel?'

'Have you any idea how difficult it is to sustain any kind of a musical career while doing residential childcare hours?'

Terri went quiet for a moment.

'From your tone, I'd guess it's not easy.'

'Well spotted. You can either meet me before or after the gig.'

'Where you playing?'

'The Phis Fliuch. On Gibson Street.'

'I'll be there by nine.'

'That gives you half an hour. We start at nine thirty sharp.'

The Phis Fliuch was a small, traditional music pub that catered for a discerning crowd of folkies, hippies and new agers. I was playing as part of a three piece, which consisted of me on strings, a virtuoso piano accordion player, who managed to add a kind of Cajun flavour even to Irish jigs and reels, and a dreadlocked English fiddle player, who liked to throw in the odd bit of gypsy jazz, which kept the sets interesting.

Terri arrived just as we were setting up. I tended to forget how striking she was, and all heads in the place turned to follow her as she came in. Tonight she had her hair tied back in a loose ponytail, and was wearing a leather jacket, baggy jeans and a PLO style scarf. I told my musical cohorts that I needed to have a quick chat with Terri, and we went into the snug.

'What's up, then?' I asked.

'Farrell has changed his plea,' Terri said.

'To what?' I asked, knowing as the words came out of my mouth that it was a question which had only one answer.

'He's pleading guilty,' Terri said.

'I don't fucking believe it,' I said. 'Sure, that's brilliant.'

'Well, there has been some bargaining and toing and froing,' Terri said. 'He's pleading to a lesser charge – four counts of incest, one count of sexual assault and the neglect is being thrown out. The state has decided not to pursue the whole abduction issue. There just isn't enough evidence. Timmy, the older brother, won't stand up in court and give evidence, which takes the claws out of his testimony.'

'How long can we expect him to go down for, then?'

'This judge is of the old school, it seems to me. The lawyer reckons he might get three or four years, probably serve two. It's not much, but . . .'

'It's crap, is what it is,' I said.

'But listen, mate, that's not the main thing.'

'Okay.'

'He wants to make a public apology to Jason.'

I thought about that one. 'Is that . . . um . . . usual?'

'Apparently it's not *un*usual in cases like this. It's a fucking trick, really, an attempt to win more sympathy, but it seems he's entitled to it.'

'All right, then. Nothing we can do about it, is there?'

Terri began to roll a cigarette, her movements jerky and agitated. I had begun to notice that she could be quite highly strung.

'It begs a question, Shane.'

'Does it?'

'Do we bring Jason in to hear this apology?'

'No,' I said immediately. It seemed a no-brainer, to me.

'Don't you think he's entitled to hear it? It might be the only one he ever gets.'

'But it doesn't mean anything,' I said. 'It's all a fucking performance.'

'I don't know,' Terri said. 'If he goes back home, the reality is that his father will be out of pokey in a couple of years, and he'll most likely be going back home himself when he's released. It might be important, that he's said sorry. Could help them build a relationship.'

I shook my head. This was all much more than I wanted to be thinking about that evening. I should have been trying to decide which song I was going to do first, and wondering about the accordion break in 'In the Jailhouse'.

'My vote is to let the kid stay at home,' I said sharply. 'I think the experience will scare the life out of him, and fill him full of guilt about the fact that his father is going to jail, a concept he is struggling to understand, anyway.'

'I think we should give it some thought,' Terri said.

'Well, that's what I think,' I said. 'Now, I've got to go and tune up.'

'All right, matey. I'll see you in the morning.'

I didn't enjoy the gig. Jason's face, racked with grief, kept swimming before my eyes.

I wasn't surprised when Sarah and I were called upstairs to the office first thing the next morning to be informed that Jason would be attending court that day.

'This is a mistake, Terri,' I said.

'I don't want to hear it. I've made my decision. It wasn't easy, and I didn't like having to do it, but there you go. I'm the manager, and those are the breaks.'

'I can't believe you're pulling rank,' I said.

'I don't really give a damn what you believe,' Terri snarled. 'Get him ready. We have to be there by mid-day.'

Two hours later Jason, dressed in his best clothes, sat between Terri and me at the front of the court. I was seething, but it was important that Jason did not pick up on any of my negative feelings. Conor sat on the other side of the room with his hot-shot lawyer, looking dapper and calm. As I watched, the solicitor whispered instructions to him, and pointed out lines highlighted in bright green on some paper attached to a clipboard.

At a little after twelve, the judge came out, and addressed the room.

'I believe we have a change of plea?'

Brian Utley stood and spoke in his booming, rapid-fire voice. 'We do indeed, Judge. My client has spent many hours considering the future of his young son, Jason, who is present in the court this morning. He has decided to plead guilty – you have the details of his plea, Judge.'

The elderly man flicked through the pages. 'And does opposing counsel accept this plea?'

'We do, Judge,' the solicitor representing Jason stood and said.

'Very well,' the judge said. 'Is there anything else before I withdraw to consider sentencing?'

'My client would like to address the court – and his son,' Utley said, his voice dripping with emotion. I shook my head bitterly.

It wasn't until Conor Farrell made his way to the witness box that Jason seemed to fully understand what was going on.

'There's my daddy,' he said loudly and cheerily, standing up on the bench and pointing at his father.

'That's right, Jase,' I said, pushing him gently to a sitting position again. 'He wants to say something. We've got to listen.'

Farrell, to my surprise, did not read from a prepared statement. He had obviously worked hard at memorizing the brief address. In fairness to him, he performed it beautifully.

'I come from a broken home, and as a young boy, I was raped and brutalized by my father,' he said, looking first to the judge, then to Jason, then across the room – he was really working the crowd. 'All I ever wanted was to have somebody tell me I was a good boy, or to notice something positive I did, or to hug me in a way that was safe and pure – sadly, nobody ever did that, for me. You see, I grew up all mixed up about how you show love to your children. I was shown the wrong way, and that's what I passed on to my kids. And I know, now, that I was wrong, very, very wrong, to have done that to my children. Jason – I love you, son –' Here, his voice broke, and tears began to stream down his smoothly shaven cheeks. 'I love you and I am so, so, sorry.'

I glanced down at Jason, and saw that his lower lip was trembling ferociously, and before I could stop him, he was up on the bench again, his hands held aloft. 'Daddy! I wants my daddy! He never done nothin' to me! I loves my daddy!'

'Oh God, I love you too, son,' Conor said.

'I feel like I'm trapped in a fucking Rocky movie,' Terri muttered as she tried to get Jason to sit. He was not prepared to acquiesce so easily this time, and I sensed that he was becoming dangerously upset. He kicked out at Terri's hands, and began to scream wordlessly. At the top of the room, Conor Farrell was trying to fight his way down to his small son, and was being restrained by uniformed Gardaí. Jason, on seeing this, began to roar and wail with renewed vigour.

'We need to get him out of here,' Terri said, as Jason grabbed a clump of her blonde tresses (she had decided to wear her hair down today – another in a series of decisions that were not working out well for her) and tugged for all he was worth.

I decided to leave my gloating to a later date, and simply nodded. Jason had lost all control, now, and was kicking and thrashing hysterically. I could hear Conor bellowing, but did not even bother to look to see how his struggle was faring. I hefted Jason over my shoulder, and carried him bodily from the room. When I had him outside the door, he seemed to sag immediately, as if all the fight had been sucked right out of him. I carried him out to the car, and, as I was strapping him into the back, he said in a little voice: 'I gonna be sick.'

I opened the door wide and stepped aside, and Jason threw up his breakfast all over the tarmac of the courtroom car park.

NOW

36

With the court case over, and Jason destined for an intensive course of group therapy, involving a strong residential aspect (he would remain in a special wing of St Phelim's for the sixteen-week duration), there was less need for me to be around him so much, and I returned to some of my other cases, which had all been placed on the back-burner as I attempted to make sense of his complex situation.

Ben remained away, and that meant I was left dealing with new referrals to the Dunleavy Trust as well, as it seemed there was an expectation from the other team-members that I would step into Ben's shoes in his absence. I was far from happy with this state of affairs, but found I had little choice as the stand-in receptionist continued to place the paperwork for these cases on my desk, even after I told her not to.

So I was very busy.

I was not allowed to visit Jason at all for the first two weeks of his programme, a policy designed to give the participants a chance to acclimatize to what was a very demanding line of treatment, so I was surprised when I got a phone call from Andrew Roche before the first week was finished.

'I'm afraid things are not working out,' Andrew said, without preamble.

I had assumed that some of the sexual offenders Roche and his team dealt with on a daily basis could be quite challenging, so I didn't know what to say to his statement initially.

'Um . . . what's wrong . . .' I said, at last. 'Is Jason not being cooperative?'

'Jason is not the problem,' Andrew Roche said. 'It's his mother.'

'Mmm,' I agreed. 'She can be difficult, all right.'

'It's not that she's proving hard to deal with,' Andrew said. 'The issue is that she hasn't turned up for the group sessions – not once.'

My heart dropped. 'Oh,' I said.

'If you can't get her to come and participate, I'm afraid that I'll have to drop Jason from the programme, and make a recommendation that he return to the normal population in St Phelim's.'

And after that, off to Salt Island, I thought.

'I'll see what I can do,' I said, and hung up.

Liz Farrell was nowhere to be found. Her neighbours informed me that she had not been about for more than a week; Rachel Keane and her colleagues at the community centre had not encountered her, and didn't know where else I should look. The couple of mobile phone numbers I had for her seemed to have been cut off.

I sat with Jason, and discussed the state of play.

'I knew this would happen,' he said. 'She has never lifted her hand to do anythin' for me, not never.'

'I'm going to keep looking for her,' I said. 'Can you think of one more place for me to try, somewhere she might only go occasionally, even? Come on, Jase, there must be somewhere we haven't looked.'

He shook his head. 'I don't really know her that well, Shane,' he said. 'Your guess is as good as mine.'

I nodded and stood up, to go and continue my search.

'You can't let me down, Shane,' Jason said as I turned to leave him. 'I won't survive in jail, so I won't. I need you to do this for me.' His voice was quiet but firm, as if he had been thinking about it long and hard.

I turned back to him. 'I'll do my best, Jason,' I said.

'I hope it's good enough,' he said and, lying down on his bed, turned his face to the wall.

My search proved utterly fruitless, and that night at nine I was parked outside Liz Farrell's home, in the dim hope that she might come home. I was on my fifteenth cigarette, Django Reinhardt playing softly on the car stereo, when a dark figure approached Liz's front door, and produced a key. I was out and over to them in a shot.

'Hey, Liz,' I said.

The figure continued to fumble with the lock. 'Lizzy ain't here,' a gruff voice replied.

'Who am I talking to?' I asked.

The person turned briefly to look at me, and I saw that this was a different lost sheep returning: Conor Farrell had come home. The years had not been kind to him – his face was deeply lined, his hair all but gone, and a heavy paunch protruded from his shirt.

In my desperation, I grasped this one straw that presented itself to me.

'Jason needs you,' I said. 'He's on a sexual offenders' programme in Phelim's, and Liz was to act as his sponsor.'

'Then talk to her,' Conor said, stepping into the dark hall. I stuck a steel-capped toe in the doorway, so he couldn't close it on me. 'Why the fuck should I help you anyway, you beardy cunt?' Conor snapped. 'I did two fuckin' years inside because of your meddlin'.'

'I have to find her.'

'Told you she'd help the boy, did she?' Conor sneered.

'Yes.'

'You promise her something?'

'That Jason could come home,' I lied.

The man laughed at that. 'Well, there's your problem. She hates him.'

This was getting me nowhere. 'Can you help me, Conor?' I pushed on. 'You'll be paid to be there.'

'Jason was a weak, snivelling kid, and he's no better now,' Conor said, and tried to close the door, cursing when the edge hit my boot.

'If he was, you were to blame,' I said. 'He was a little boy, and you abused his trust.'

'Ah, he was never any good,' Conor barked. 'Why do you think I had to look outside the house for my jollies? He couldn't take it. Cryin' and whinin' like a girl. Fuckin' pathetic.'

I wanted to grab the man and kick him until something broke, but it would get me nowhere. 'Well, he learned all your tricks,' I said. 'But it's not too late, for him. He could still be turned around.'

Conor smiled, and it was not a pleasant sight. 'Who'd find little ones for me, then?' he said, and I suddenly wanted to sit down very badly. I realized that Jason's attempted abduction of the girl out playing had a whole new depth of meaning.

'I can see I'm wasting my time,' I said, and went to go back to my car. 'I will be informing the police of our conversation, of course.'

'Inform away, you thick bollix,' Farrell said. 'I don't shit on my own doorstep any more.'

226

And he closed the door. I sat back in the Austin and realized, finally, that the last die had been rolled for Jason Farrell, and his luck had all run out.

37

Jason was crying. I sat across from him, holding his hand. He pulled it away from me angrily.

'You said you'd fix this,' he said.

'I said I'd do my best,' I said. 'That's not the same thing.'

'I won't stay here!'

'You don't have any choice,' I said. 'If you do manage to get away, they'll bring you back.'

Jason curled up in a ball, and leaned against the wall.

'I don't got no one,' he said, almost to himself. 'I never did have. When I was in res with you, and Terri and all, that was good for a while, but sure I messed that up, too.'

'You were only little,' I said. 'You can't be blamed for that not working out.'

'If they don't let me out of here, I'll top meself.'

'They won't let that happen,' I said.

'Just you wait and see.'

'You've got to ride this out, Jason,' I said. 'It doesn't have to be the end of your life. You're still very young, and you can make your time work for you. Go to school, get some qualifications . . . I'll come and see you as often as I can.'

I stayed with him for another hour, but he remained firm in his resolve. He would not accept this turn of events, and if the situation did not change, he would simply take matters into his own hands.

I told Garry Timmons, who was, once again, in charge of Jason's welfare, about the boy's suicide threat, and went back to the office. I had a ton of files waiting for me.

THEN

38

Fionn Jackson, Jason's social worker, was meeting Jason for the second time. I sat on the couch in the living room, occasionally rephrasing things that were said so that Jason could understand what he was being told. I wondered just how much time Fionn actually spent with the many children I knew were on his books.

'I gonna go home?' Jason asked, looking to me to confirm what had just been said.

'In a little while,' I said, wanting to stress that this would not happen that day, or the next.

'Would you like to live with your mammy again?' Fionn asked.

'Yeah!' Jason said, plainly delighted. 'Live with my mammy and Shane and Sarah!'

The social worker looked at me as if he had just encountered a strange breed of child for the first time, and had no idea what to do with it.

'No, Jase, you could still visit us here, but you'd sleep in your old home, with your mum,' I said.

'She no lock me up, righ'?' Jason said.

'No, that won't happen any more,' I said.

Fionn Jackson spoke to me in the driveway before he drove off.

'I'd like regular access visits established, building up in a few weeks' time to weekends away,' he said. 'I'd like to see this brought to a close before six months are up.'

'Might that be rushing things?' I asked.

'I don't think so. As far as we know, Liz had no part in the abuse.'

'Neglect is a form of abuse, Fionn,' I said. 'She didn't wash him or feed him, or put clothes on his back. He was barely potty-trained when he came here.'

Fionn nodded. 'I've read the file, Shane,' he said. 'Don't you think she deserves a chance?'

'Yes, when she's proven she's worthy of one. And I don't think we'll know that for sure in six months.'

'We'll just have to watch this space, won't we?' Fionn said.

It was as if all Jason's Christmases had come at once. Every conversation was littered with references to 'going home to live with my mammy'. The other children got quite sick of it, and began to mimic, but he didn't seem to care. He would laugh at Ellen when she screwed up her face to replicate his little-old-man appearance, and join in with her as she repeated the mantra: *I'm goin' home to live with my mammy*. The girl had become quite fond of Jason, by then, and such a game would always end with them both in guffaws of laughter.

The laughter came to an end when Liz was due to pick Jason up for the first of their access visits, and didn't show. Jason sat on the front doorstep waiting for her for two hours, refusing to come in until it got too cold, even for him. I rang Liz's number again and again, but all to no avail.

This setback seemed not to dampen Jason's enthusiasm for his imminent move, and the following Saturday, when he was due to go out with Liz the second time, he was, again, in position on the doorstep at the appointed time, ready to greet her. Again, he waited in vain. In frustration, I asked Terri if we could drive over to the Farrell house, to see what was going on.

Terri agreed. We drove out of the city and along the narrow, winding roads where the Farrells lived before they moved into the Oldtown.

The house was dark and empty. As I stood at the front door, an old man shuffling past on the lane in front of the house called to me: 'You won't get an answer in there, boy.'

'Why not?' I called back.

'They all moved away.'

'When are they coming back?'

The man shrugged. 'I don't know. Maybe not never.'

When we got back to The Crow's Nest, I called Fionn and suggested he try and find out Liz's whereabouts.

'That's hardly my job, now is it?' he said.

'You told Jason he was moving back home with his mother,' I said. 'Now it seems his mother has done a bunk. I think that makes it your job.'

'Oh,' he said. 'I see.'

Initially, Jason took the news that Liz had disappeared quite well, or so it seemed. We waited for two weeks, until it looked certain that she was not coming back any time soon, before telling him that there had been a change of plan. He sat in silence as Fionn broke the news, then went out to play with Albert. An hour later, he came back in and sat down in the playroom.

'You okay, Jason?' I asked.

'Yeah,' came the response.

Twenty minutes later, there was a knock on the door. Albert's mother was furious: Jason had bitten her son, and drawn blood. She was on her way to the hospital with him, and wanted us to know that she expected the Health Board to pay any resultant bills.

'And I will not be permitting my son to play with that animal any more,' she said as she stormed off.

So began a gradual deterioration in Jason's behaviour. It started with his being short-tempered, lashing out whenever he felt slighted or upset, but within a week, the other children had returned to giving him a wide berth. I also noticed his speech becoming monosyllabic. It seemed that he was regressing, and regressing fast.

Things came to a head one afternoon when Jason, without warning, attacked Leo as he played in the garden. Jason was holding a sharp piece of rock in his hand, and used it like a blade. If Sarah had not been there, Leo could have been badly hurt.

A case conference was called. The assorted staff of The Crow's Nest, as well as Fionn and a psychologist who had assessed Jason on his being taken into care, gathered in a room in the Health Board offices.

'We've given it a go,' Terri said. 'And I have to tell you, I think we've run out of rope on this one. I'm recommending that Jason be sent somewhere he will not pose a risk to other kids, and where there are enough staff to cope with him.'

'A place has come up in a High Support Unit in Kells,' the psychologist said. 'It seems from the behaviour described, that they might be better suited to deal with him.'

'All agreed, then?' Fionn asked.

I sat there, unable to say a word. I was devastated, but in my heart knew that The Crow's Nest was not a safe place for Jason any more. 'Is this a short-term thing?' I asked, finally. 'I mean, will he be coming back to us?'

'That depends on Jason,' Fionn said, and that was that.

They took him on a rainy afternoon a fortnight later. He fought them all the way out to the ambulance that would take him to his new home. He had stopped speaking again by this time, and I caught his eye for a moment as he was carried out of the door. I was reminded of when he had attacked Yolanda, his social worker, on his first day. All I saw was grief and pain and madness. I could still hear him screaming as the vehicle pulled out of the gate. When I could no longer see the ambulance, I made my way upstairs to the small office, sat down at the desk, and cried.

That night, I saw the Red Lady again. Leo had been disturbed by nightmares, as he sometimes was, and I was sitting on the carpet near his doorway, waiting for him to drift back to sleep, when she walked past me. I saw her in the corner of my eye, a rose-coloured apparition moving down the hallway in the darkness. She turned to look at me, and I saw her huge dark eyes for a moment, and then she was gone.

The next morning, I told Terri I was quitting. The Crow's Nest had lost all joy for me.

NOW

39

Ben Tyrrell returned to work three weeks after Jason was sent to Salt Island – which took place on his seventeenth birthday: a bitter gift if ever there was one. Jason had reverted to silence, and my visits with him pretty much involved me talking, and him glowering at me. He was on suicide watch, as he'd tried to hang himself with his bed sheets on his first day. During his second week, I was told he had taken my name from his visitors' list: Jason was freezing me out.

As it happened I was sitting in his office when Ben arrived back at work, going through some books on policy and procedure.

'Don't get too comfortable in here,' he said jovially as he came in through the door. 'I'm back.'

I put down what I had been reading. 'It's good to see you, Ben,' I said – and I meant it.

He sat in the chair he usually kept for clients, or for when one of us dropped in for a chat. 'How have you been, Shane?'

'Not so good,' I admitted.

'Anything I can do?'

I smiled. 'Yeah, there is one thing.'

'Name it.'

'You can accept my resignation.'

Ben sat back, looking saddened and hurt.

'Is this over Jason Farrell? Because if it is, I can assure

you the past weeks have simply been a horrible mess that will never happen again . . .'

'I don't blame you for what happened to Jason,' I said. 'I was mad at you for bailing out on me, but the truth is, that boy was on a path towards disaster long before he walked into Dunleavy House. He was already headed that way when I met him ten years ago, if I'm honest. He could have been diverted, and set right, if the system had worked. But it didn't. You told me it was too late for him when he burst in on us and hit Mrs Munro, and you were right. I was just so caught up in my own grief at the loss of him years ago, and the part I played in it, that I couldn't hear you.'

'So you made some mistakes,' Ben said. 'We all do, from time to time. Stay. Learn. Help me to be stronger, too – I know I let you down, and I want to put that right.'

'I need to do something else for a while,' I said. 'This has taken over my life, and I need a break. I'm sorry, Ben.'

'You're part of a team, here, Shane,' Ben said. 'We need you.'

'I'm not irreplaceable,' I said. 'There are plenty of other people who can do what I do – maybe even do it better. You'll fill the gap, and in three months, you'll have forgotten I was ever here.'

'And what is to become of Jason, then? Are you walking away from him, after all this?'

I smiled, sadly. It was a valid question. 'Karl Devereux has some contacts on the inside on The Shaker. He's making sure Jason doesn't come to any harm from . . . er . . . external sources.'

'You mean that he doesn't get beaten up or raped.'

'Yes. He's on suicide watch, anyway, and he refuses to

see me – I'm not sure there's much else I can do. I'm going to check in with the staff from time to time, but he's closed the door on me. He feels I let him down badly. That I made him promises I couldn't keep.'

'You didn't, though.'

I paused to think about that. 'Ben, I just don't know. I review this case in my head, going right back to when I met him first when he was only a little kid, and I wonder if there aren't a hundred things I should have done differently. Should I have insisted social workers try harder to find his mother when she ran off? Should I have spoken up when they were sending him to that High Support Unit? Should I have just prepared him for prison this time around from the beginning, and not offered him hope? I don't know. What I do know is that he has benefited not one micron from having me in his life.'

'That's not true,' Ben said, gently.

'I think it is.'

We said nothing for a few moments.

'So you're leaving us,' Ben said, finally.

'Yes.'

'I can't get you to change your mind?'

'No. I've told my landlord that I'm moving out. I'm going to try moving to the country for a while. I lived there before, and I think I liked it.'

'You're leaving the city?'

'For a while.'

Ben nodded slowly. 'And what will you do?'

'I was thinking of just playing music for a living. Pubs and that. I might do a little part-time carework here and there, to make ends meet, but I think I'm just going to be a musician.'

'That's not steady work – you know that.'

'I'll get by.'

'I can see you've made your mind up,' Ben said.

'I have.'

'We'll miss you here. I'll miss you.'

'You'll get over it,' I grinned.

And he did, too.

Afterword

I never saw Jason Farrell again. I heard on the grapevine (from Rachel Keane, in fact) that he had survived his time (eighteen months, in total) on The Shaker and, on his release, returned to his haunts in the Oldtown. Rachel informs me that he is actively involved in organized crime, but that no complaints about him as a sexual predator have been brought to her attention.

I don't know if that is progress or not. Perhaps it is a kind of development.

I did not return to Dunleavy House, except to visit occasionally. I am still in touch with Ben Tyrrell, and, although our relationship continues to be a volatile one, I consider him a close and valued friend.

The children from The Crow's Nest have all done well, in their way. Ellen leads a relatively normal life, although she still battles with her inner demons. Leo is in college now. Mark works as a personal trainer, and is very successful.

Terri returned to Australia six years after I left The Crow's Nest, and is still there. I spoke to Sarah the other day, and she is still working in social care, and is as much a joy as she ever was. She is married and has her own children, and is very happy.

Darren is in Australia, now, too – he moved there recently, with his family, after many years at the coalface of child protection in Ireland. He is involved in youth work.

The Red Lady, according to an historian I consulted some years later, was the daughter of a man who owned The Crow's Nest at the end of the nineteenth century. She was a renowned beauty, the toast of the locality, who died of pneumonia when she was only twenty-one. She had, by all accounts, lived a sad life, and there were rumours her father did not treat her well – he was waiting for her to marry well, so that she might support his gambling habit.

I have only been back to The Crow's Nest once in the years since I left, and I did not go inside. I stood in the park across the road and looked up at the old building, so full of memories, laughter and pain. A family lives there, now, and I listened to the children playing in the garden, and thought, just for a second, that I caught a glimpse of red from the living-room window. I waited, to see if I might catch it again, but she was gone, like an autumn leaf on the wind – fragile and transitory.

He just wanted a decent book to read ...

Not too much to ask, is it? It was in 1935 when Allen Lane, Managing Director of Bodley Head Publishers, stood on a platform at Exeter railway station looking for something good to read on his journey back to London. His choice was limited to popular magazines and poor-quality paperbacks – the same choice faced every day by the vast majority of readers, few of whom could afford hardbacks. Lane's disappointment and subsequent anger at the range of books generally available led him to found a company – and change the world.

'We believed in the existence in this country of a vast reading public for intelligent books at a low price, and staked everything on it'
Sir Allen Lane, 1902–1970, founder of Penguin Books

The quality paperback had arrived – and not just in bookshops. Lane was adamant that his Penguins should appear in chain stores and tobacconists, and should cost no more than a packet of cigarettes.

Reading habits (and cigarette prices) have changed since 1935, but Penguin still believes in publishing the best books for everybody to enjoy. We still believe that good design costs no more than bad design, and we still believe that quality books published passionately and responsibly make the world a better place.

So wherever you see the little bird – whether it's on a piece of prize-winning literary fiction or a celebrity autobiography, political tour de force or historical masterpiece, a serial-killer thriller, reference book, world classic or a piece of pure escapism – you can bet that it represents the very best that the genre has to offer.

Whatever you like to read – trust Penguin.

read more
www.penguin.co.uk